D1348337

BURRELL

A PORTRAIT OF A COLLECTOR

Sir William Burrell at the age of about sixty, taken by the well-known Glasgow firm of photographers, T. & R. Annan.

RICHARD MARKS

BURRELL

A PORTRAIT OF A COLLECTOR
Sir William Burrell 1861–1958

RICHARD DREW PUBLISHING
– Glasgow –

First published 1983 by
Richard Drew Publishing Ltd
20 Park Circus, Glasgow G3 6BE
Scotland

Copyright © Richard Marks 1983

The publisher acknowledges
the financial assistance
of the Scottish Arts Council
in the publication of this book

British Library Cataloguing in Publication Data

Marks, Richard
Burrell.
1. Burrell, Sir William   2. Art patrons
——Biography
I. Title
338.7'61'700924   NX712.B/

ISBN 0-86267-033-0
ISBN 0-86267-037-3 Pbk

Editor: Antony Kamm
Designed by James W Murray
Index by Patricia Bascom

Printed and bound in Great Britain by Robert Hartnoll Ltd., Bodmin
Colour printing by Wood Westworth & Co. Ltd, St Helens
Set in Baskerville by John Swain & Son, Glasgow
Colour Reproduction by Ardroit Photo Litho Limited, Birmingham
Black & White Reproduction by Morrison Scott Studios, Limited, Crawley, Sussex

IN MEMORIAM

—

JEANNIE EILEEN MARKS
† *17 August 1979*

WILLIAM HENRY MARKS
† *25 December 1982*

CONTENTS

LIST OF COLOUR PLATES

FOREWORD

by Peter Wilson, Honorary Life President of Sotheby's

WHEN this year the Sir William Burrell collection is shown to the public for the first time it will be possible to see one of the most remarkable assemblage of works of art ever brought together by one man.

Burrell himself told me that as a boy he used to buy an occasional picture attributed to Raeburn at a Glasgow saleroom, but he always had a good look at the frame to try and avoid spending the few pounds available to him without, as it were, hedging his bet. In buying portraits by Raeburn almost a hundred years ago he was going along with the taste of his time. But soon he began to purchase incomparable works by Degas and other French artists of the 19th century. His real love was for Gothic Art, and especially Gothic tapestries, of which he formed a collection only surpassed by that of the Metropolitan Museum.

As an old man, in the late 1940's, he became an avid collector of antiquities. It can truly be said that no collector of his generation enjoyed more eclectic tastes, and certainly no collector with comparable financial resources was able to throw his net wider and to amass over a period of almost eighty years a more impressive assemblage of works of art.

The J.P. Morgans, the Clarence Mackays and others during the decades when Sir William was forming his collection were able to bring together superb masterpieces beyond his reach, but the Burrell Collection can truly be said to hold its own in any company. It will be seen by the public as a remarkable manifestation of one man's taste, culture, knowledge, canniness and appreciation of so many and such varied civilisations; a truly remarkable achievement for a collector in great measure relying on his own judgment and sensitivity, which faltered so seldom, over a vast field ranging from incomparable examples of painting, textiles and sculpture to the humblest artifact.

Clearly this museum cannot begin to compete with the most sublime monument to a single man – the Frick Collection – but as far as Britain is concerned there is nothing comparable.

Now that at last the Collection has become available for display, in a gallery especially designed to house it, there is no doubt that great numbers of visitors will derive pleasure of a very special kind. It will be impossible for anyone to enter the gallery for the first time without wondering about the personality of the collector. Perhaps his eyes will be opened to a branch of art previously unknown to him. It is to be hoped that over the years many young people will be inspired to appreciate and possibly even to collect works of art (some of them even today are not expensive) the love of which adds so much to the enjoyment of life.

PETER WILSON
Château de Clavary
July 1983

PREFACE

WHATEVER reception this book may have, it is tolerably certain that Sir William Burrell would not have welcomed it: he was a private man who abhorred publicity. His probable reaction can be gauged from a letter written in 1946 to Tom Honeyman, the Director of Glasgow Museums and Art Galleries at the time Burrell gave the Collection to the city, about an approach from a journal to write an article on his reminiscences as a collector:

> If anyone approaches you at any time with such a suggestion I beg that you kindly let them know it is quite impossible. For any experiences to appear in print would be repugnant to me.

On another occasion he said that it was the collection, not the collector, that was the important thing. The two are, of course, so intimately related that it is impossible to discuss the one without the other. Moreover Burrell has been the subject of much interest and speculation, like so many public figures who by their very efforts to avoid the glare of publicity only succeed in attracting it, and it seems an appropriate moment to set the record as straight as possible. A conscious effort has been made to let the man speak for himself from his letters and notes.

There are certain obstacles to writing a biography of Sir William Burrell, stemming largely from his own reticence. Although much correspondence and detailed notes on his acquisitions exist, the coverage is by no means complete: primary materials for the first half of his life (and particularly his childhood) are very sparse. Again, much more is known about his art collecting than his activities as a very successful ship-owner.

That there are not more errors and omissions is due to the assistance of many individuals. It is a very pleasant task to record the author's gratitude to those who have been so generous with help. Bill Wells must be singled out for particular mention: without his excellent recording of the Collection and assiduous pursuit of primary material this account would not have been possible. It is really he and not this writer who is the best-equipped to compile Burrell's life. To Rosemary Scott, Jimmy Thomson and Philip Vainker, the author's colleagues on the staff of the Burrell Collection, thanks are due for their patient answering of queries on the sections of the Collection of which they have specialist knowledge. David Burrell, Dr John Cage and Gerry Cassidy were invaluable guides to the shipping world of the late nineteenth and early twentieth centuries and Dr Peter Savage's unrivalled knowledge of Burrell's dealings with Robert Lorimer was especially helpful. I am also indebted to the following who all provided material: Hugh Brigstocke, Meg Buchanan, Dr Ronald Cant, Leslie Dawson, Michael Donnelly, the Rt Hon the Viscount Eccles, Mandy Green, J.A. Houston, Mrs Gertrude Hunt, Christopher Lorimer, Ms A.B. Miller, the Rt Hon the Viscount Muirshiel, John Partridge, Dick Randall, Sheena Smith, Hugh Stevenson, Mrs Frank Surgey, Patrick Taylor, Dr Colin Thompson, Mrs Julia Turbitt, Peter Vaughan, Frank Whyte and Arnold Zwemmer. Not least has been the co-operation of Sir William Burrell's surviving relatives, whose anecdotes and reminiscences have done so much to put flesh on to the bare bones of this account: to single out some would be doing an injustice to others. Mention must, however, be made of Merrick Mitchell, who laboured unceasingly to find a home for his uncle's collection, of which he was a Trustee. It is a particular matter of regret to me that he did not live to see his work finally bear fruit. In no sense can any of the above-named be held responsible for errors of fact or interpretation: those rest entirely with the author.

As for the labours involved in editing the manuscript of this book only Antony Kamm is able to speak; this writer is deeply grateful for his advice and encouragement.

Finally I must as always pay tribute to the assistance, tangible and intangible, given by my wife Rita. Without it this book would not have been written.

INTRODUCTION

BURRELL THE COLLECTOR

Whatever happens it should be a consolation for you to know that your colln. will give pleasure to future generations.

Wilfred Drake

IN common with other wealthy men Burrell preserved his privacy as well as he did his health. He was a man of complex personality, but one who was careful to conceal his innermost emotions. There are no clues to be found in his childhood or adolescence which provide the keys to his adult behaviour like those seized upon by Orson Welles and used so effectively in his portrait of William Randolph Hearst in *Citizen Kane*. Burrell steadfastly refused to reveal anything about his origins, commercial and family life. His letters are equally uninformative. Their prosaic, business-like tone gives little away. Only very occasionally is there anything approaching a flight of poetic fantasy or an expression of aesthetic appreciation. Ironically his posthumous reputation has suffered from this deliberate self-effacement. One acquaintance has even gone so far as to state that Burrell was singularly devoid of human feelings. No-one else has repeated this harsh judgement, but the popularly held opinion was that he was a ruthless and dour old miser. There is rarely smoke without fire, but this is an over-simplification. Moreover it has to be borne in mind that many of the stories which have led to this image date from Burrell's declining years when certain aspects of his character became exaggerated; there are few individuals of great age who do not develop peculiar fetishes and foibles. Those who knew him before his last years and his most intimate acquaintances tend to give a rather different account.

Notwithstanding Burrell's own silence and the gaps in one's knowledge, there is still much that can be said with some degree of conviction, not least because of the strong element of consistency in his behaviour throughout his life. Although at the age of fourteen he joined a firm which was already prospering, his father and grandfather had known hard times and Burrell never broke out of the mould of personal frugality and awareness of the need to watch over the pennies which was set in his early years. He was a typical example of that well-known phenomenon, the generous benefactor who lived in private penury. As he moved towards old age his penny-pinching in certain respects reached absurd lengths. He was moreover a stern man, uncompromising and unforgiving. Some of those who knew him well maintain that there was no charity in him. Certainly he never suffered fools gladly and rarely were those who crossed him ever restored to favour. Tom Honeyman doubted whether anyone outside his family ever influenced him. He was a man of strongly held views and with a firm belief in his own judgement. Once he had made up his mind that was it. When on the rare occasions he did ask for someone else's opinion he was usually looking for confirmation of his own views rather than opposition! Honeyman was but one amongst a whole host of individuals and public bodies who fell foul of him. He set high standards for himself and expected the same from everyone else.

Yet there was a lighter side to Burrell's nature. Contrary to his reserved and austere image he had a keen, if dry, sense of humour which by all accounts he retained throughout his life. Moreover in spite of his reluctance to recount his experiences as a successful businessman and collector, once coaxed out of his shell he could be an immensely entertaining raconteur, as A.J. McNeill Reid recalled:

> I have had most entertaining times with him. I remember a journey with him to Paris many years ago. He started telling stories at Victoria and never stopped till we reached Paris.

Such a strong-willed character could never have been easy with whom to live. His wife and daughter undoubtedly suffered in certain respects, even though he was devoted to them. From his childhood he was imbued with a strong sense of moral rectitude, not to say primness, and not a hint of impropriety has filtered through from any source. By all accounts he treated his employees, whether in the family business or at Hutton Castle, fairly according to the lights of his time. He was no worse than many of the great *entrepreneurs* of Victorian Glasgow and considerably better than some. If he did not have the social conscience displayed by the arms and armour enthusiast R.L. Scott, who gave up collecting during the Great Depression of the 1930's in order to keep on the workforce in his shipbuilding yards, he was public-spirited enough to try and do something about the city's appalling housing problems in the early years of the century. Former office boys employed by Burrell and Son remember him in a favourable light. One of them, orphaned at the age of fourteen, recalls that when he enlisted in the army in 1914

Burrell promised him half his salary to augment his military pay if he became an officer (a dubious privilege considering the mortality rate amongst the commissioned ranks) and he was as good as his word. He was always a believer in the old virtues of hard work and self-advancement. The domestic servants at Hutton Castle in the inter-war years may have worked long hours and received the usual low pay, but Burrell at least ensured that they were provided with decent accommodation and facilities. Most of those in the art world with whom he had dealings for any length of time respected and liked him. He may have haggled over prices but he paid his bills promptly and knew what he was doing. Counter-balancing those with whom he fell out were individuals who retained his confidence and whose relations with him extended beyond those normal between business associates. To some intimates he could be thoughtful and generous.

In business affairs Burrell was little short of a genius, allied to which was that essential ingredient for success, good fortune. When he and his brother George took over on the death of their father in 1885, the family

Sir William Burrell's father William (1832–85).

(left) Sir William Burrell's brother George as a young man. The portrait belonged to his grandson, the late George Burrell McKean.

firm though prospering was not to be numbered in the first rank of Clyde-based shipping companies. The world of marine commerce was a hard one, but within a few years the Burrell brothers by shrewd planning and enterprise allied to breathtaking opportunism gained an international reputation. It was an ideal combination: George was the technical expert, keeping abreast of developments in marine engineering, and William had the financial and managerial flair. The latter in particular had an eye for detail and a methodical approach which he never lost, even after his retirement from the shipping business. Their formula for success was simple but demanded ice-cool nerve.

There were many opportunities for the enterprising and hard-working in late nineteenth and early twentieth-century Glasgow, and Burrell was but one of many who prospered. Moreover individuals rarely win lasting fame for their achievements in the arena of commerce and Burrell is no exception to this rule. Few traces remain today as reminders of the source of his wealth. The last of the ships which once flew the house flag of Burrell and Son went to the breakers' yard years ago. The premises in George Square occupied by the firm in its most prosperous years have been demolished and its other offices in Buchanan Street and St Vincent Street have long since been converted to other uses. Port Dundas, where Burrell's grandfather first established himself, is an unhappy conglomeration of stagnant pools, decaying warehouses and modern commercial premises.

The private residences of the family have also largely lost all connections with their past occupants. Burrell's modest first home in Scotia Street was bulldozed during the massive re-developments which transformed Glasgow in the 1960's; his next residence at Willowbank Street still stands, occupied by immigrants to the city from much further afield than Northumberland, the county of origin of the Burrell family. The imposing house in Devonshire Gardens is now converted into flats and 8 Great Western Terrace has been given over to welfare purposes, although its earlier affiliations are acknowledged by the name 'Burrell House'. Even Hutton Castle, for which Burrell paid a high price (and not just in financial terms) in order to turn it into his ideal baronial mansion, has been abandoned and is a depressing half-ruin.

Immortality is more readily obtained by forming an art collection and handing it over to public ownership. It is for this that Burrell is remembered. The amassing of a vast art collection was his great passion and in presenting it to the City of Glasgow he joined the ranks of the greatest benefactors to the nation's cultural life. In bringing together the Collection he applied the principles he had learned in the shipping world to the art market. He loved haggling and always kept a weather eye out for a bargain. Chiefly because they attracted large prices Burrell usually avoided making bulk purchases from well-known

The end of an ideal: Hutton Castle in 1982.

collections. In this he differed from the likes of J. Pierpont Morgan, Randolph Hearst and the Belgian butter magnate, Mayer van den Bergh. When he did so he often went to considerable lengths to put off potential rivals by instructing several different agents to bid on his behalf. He derived as much enjoyment from the pursuit of a work of art as he did from concluding a successful commercial transaction. Unlike many of his wealthy fellow-collectors, particularly those who were Duveen's clients, he did not forget all the lessons he had learned in the harsh world of business.

His upbringing and career naturally drew Burrell to the man of business in the art world rather than the academic. Although he employed specialist art historians such as Professor Yetts and Dr Kurth to vet and catalogue objects in his collection, on the whole he eschewed the advice of this species when it came to purchasing. In this respect he differed from Robert von Hirsch, whose magnificent collection of medieval art was largely formed under the guidance of Georg Swarzenski, the Director of the Städelsches Kunstinstitut at Frankfurt am Main. Burrell considered that dealers were more likely to be reliable as they could be held accountable for mistakes. Amongst the large numbers of art dealers whom he used during his long career as a collector there existed an inner group of trusted advisers. He was never an easy man with whom to deal and more than occasionally he must have been infuriating. Yet most of the members of the 'inner sanctum' liked and respected him; he was fair with them and in their turn they served him well.

How good a collector was Burrell? This is the question that is invariably asked and it is one to which it is not easy to give a straight-forward answer. Having left school at an early age he always lacked a scholarly background. He was never interested in filling the gaps in his knowledge by reading and consequently failed to equip himself with a library commensurate with his collection. Unlike W.L. Hildburgh and Philip Nelson, the only other contemporary British collectors of medieval art of any standing, he never published anything on the objects in his possession, although he was always pleased when some-one else did. Had he known more he might have avoided a few mistakes. Burrell sought to overcome this handicap by travelling and seeing as much as possible. Moreover his phenomenal memory and eye for quality were assets of which he made full use. All those who knew him well speak of his ability to examine prospective purchases critically; not for him the Randolph Hearst practice of accumulation without in many instances knowing what was in his collection. Lord Clark described Burrell as having a strong plastic sense and the hands of a sculptor and summed him up:

He was not simply an amasser; he was an aesthete.

It is not difficult to pick holes in Burrell's collecting. He has been accused of spreading his net too widely; had he confined himself to fewer areas he could have formed a stronger, if narrower, collection. It has even been said that he was indiscriminate and amassed a wide variety of objects without any consideration of planning (it is statements such as these which have given rise to the convenient label of 'the Millionaire Magpie'). Another common pronouncement has been that he would have bought better if he had not always been so keen on a bargain. None of these observations is totally without validity, but they have not in most instances been based on detailed knowledge of the Collection and the issue needs a more careful analysis than it has hitherto received.

Burrell is not to be numbered among collectors who were ahead of their time in their interests. He was never a leader of taste, nor a supporter of the *avant-garde*. Whichever of his interests is examined, invariably someone else can be found who was collecting in that field before him. This statement applies as much locally as internationally. Burrell's own assertion notwithstanding, he was not the first Scottish collector to buy the works of Degas and in spite of Alex Reid's promptings he never developed a liking for the *plein-air* Impressionist painters such as Monet, Pissarro and Sisley; he was equally blind to the attractions of the Post-Impressionists: with the exception of a handful of works the artists of these schools are not represented in the Burrell Collection, although they were taken up by other Scottish collectors.

Like everyone, Burrell had his own likes and dislikes in art. He was always attracted more by vigour, strong colours (particularly in stained glass) and strength of line rather than elaboration and delicacy. The comparative simplicity of the early Chinese ceramics and bronzes, and of the Gothic art of Northern Europe, appealed more to his austere nature than the frivolities of Baroque and Rococo: in his purchases of late seventeenth and early eighteenth-century art he confined himself to the restrained fields of British portraiture, furniture and silver, together with a few ceramics. Neither did the art of Renaissance Italy ever find much favour in his eyes. Possibly he was put off at an early stage by Joseph Duveen's enthusiasm for it and his correspondingly high prices, but he was always by temperament and inclination a Northerner. He did make a few good purchases in this field, like the Bellini *Virgin and Child*, but even here he had to be led to the trough by Lord Clark and a major factor in his decision to drink was the bargain price. *See plate 1*

Even within his favourite fields Burrell had his prejudices. He evinced little interest in illuminated manuscripts and much preferred the colourful heraldic glass of the early sixteenth century to the contemporary Flemish figural roundels. His attention was firmly focussed on medieval art of the period 1300–1530 and it was only with the greatest difficulty he could be persuaded to buy the occasional Romanesque piece: in the case of the *Temple Pyx* the vendors were reduced to appealing to his patriotic dislike of seeing works of art leaving the British Isles for the New World. It may be remarked in passing that the traffic was not invariably one way: there are a large number of items which Burrell acquired from American collectors, including Randolph Hearst. *See plate 19*

Amongst his large collection of Chinese ceramics there is not one example of *famille rose* porcelain of the eighteenth century onwards. It is also rather surprising in view of his interest in heraldry that he should have ignored almost completely Chinese armorial porcelain made for the European export market. Equally remarkable, in the light of his taste for the Hague and Barbizon schools, is the absence of Dutch seventeenth-century landscape painting from the Collection.

In contrast with the omissions and equally regretted by the curator are those instances where Burrell over-collected. There are several areas where the cry can be raised – if only he had not acquired so many examples of such-and-such but had applied the resources to filling some of the gaps. These include the English alabaster carvings, of which there are nearly fifty in the Collection, and even more to the English furniture and silver of the seventeenth and eighteenth centuries, although much of it was intended for domestic use at Hutton. The worst example of all is the proliferation of Chinese brightly coloured over-glazed enamel wares of the same period as the furniture and silver. It can even be claimed that Burrell bought too many pictures by Degas (there are 22 in the Collection), not all of them first-class. Here the accusation that the Collection suffers from Burrell's constant hunger for art at bargain prices can be levelled with some justification. There are certain categories which although strong in quantity are sparse in pieces of outstanding merit: English eighteenth-century silver immediately comes to mind. The medieval sculpture likewise includes few masterpieces. Furthermore the list of very desirable objects which Burrell is known to have had the chance of acquiring and failed to because he thought they were too expensive makes sad reading. Equally regrettable are the sales of a number of first-rate pictures. Several were in part-exchange for new acquisitions, but it is difficult to avoid the conclusion that the incentive behind the sale of the Whistlers and several other paintings in the early 1900's was the knowledge that the profits would be considerable.

Taking each section of the Collection individually it is not difficult to find weaknesses. There *are* fakes and pieces which have been over-restored, there *are* gaps and omissions and there *are* over-concentrations. It is also quite easy to name better contemporary collectors within each field. In that of Chinese ceramics Burrell comes some way behind Sir Percival David and George Eumorfopolous, to name but two. As a collector of paintings he is surpassed by many, especially by Joseph Duveen's American clients like Frick, Kress and Andrew Mellon. Similarly there were greater collectors of medieval art: Henry Walters and Robert von Hirsch acquired superior individual objects and on a more modest scale Hildburgh had a larger and more comprehensive collection of English alabasters.

But to emphasise the deficiencies in each section is to lose sight of the whole, and this is how the Collection must be viewed. There are few collectors who can stand comparison with Burrell in scope and breadth. He succeeded in forming a major collection in almost every field in which he was interested. The Chinese ceramics and bronzes are only surpassed by three or four other museums in the United Kingdom and the Persian, Indian and Caucasian rugs and carpets can be ranked with the holdings of the Victoria and Albert Museum. Burrell's paintings, particularly those of the French nineteenth-century period, would grace any major gallery. Even the Ancient Civilisations, one of the less strong sections, contains some outstanding pieces and within the con-

Three examples from the collection of ancient artefacts:
Etruscan earthenware female head of the 3rd century BC (above left).
Attic earthenware drinking-cup, c. 500 BC (above right).
Fragment of a Roman mosaic pavement of the 1st century BC (right).

fines of Scotland is of outstanding importance. And all this is before the chief strength of Burrell's collection, the Late Gothic and Early Renaissance works of art from Northern Europe, is taken into account. He managed to amass a collection of medieval stained glass which stands comparison with the holdings of the Victoria and Albert Museum and the Cloisters in New York. The tapestries also rank amongst the world's finest collections (Burrell himself considered that the tapestries were by far the most valuable part of the Collection). The late medieval collections as a whole, i.e. including the architectural and large-scale sculpture, ivories and enamels, are only surpassed in their comprehensiveness within the United Kingdom by the Victoria and Albert

Burrell's most expensive tapestry: the Franco-Burgundian GRAPE HARVEST of c. 1450–75, purchased in 1927 for £12,600. See also plate 3.

Museum. To speak of the Collection in the same breath as these great international institutions gives some measure of Burrell's achievement. The holdings of such bodies have been built up over many decades through numerous benefactions and the labours of generations of specialist curatorial staff, and in some cases with the aid of vast funds. By contrast the Burrell Collection was formed by one individual lacking in academic knowledge and with comparatively limited resources. The last point needs emphasising, for although Burrell was wealthy he did not enjoy the huge financial resources of American collectors such as Widener, Frick, Pierpont Morgan, Kress, Mellon and Hearst; he could never compete with the likes of Pierpont Morgan, who could afford to splash out $750,000 on works of art within the space of two months in 1906. In the 46 years for which records exist Burrell only spent an average of £20,000 per annum.

It is against this background that Burrell's pursuit of bargains must be seen. He haggled partly because this was his natural instinct but also because of force of circumstance. He was able to amass a collection which from the 1930's could stand comparison with the great accumulations of the American art magnates only by dint of careful planning and organisation, by shrewd selection of his agents and judgement of the market.

Burrell was far from being 'the Millionaire Magpie'. At quite an early stage he had defined his collecting interests and adhered to them for the rest of his life; the only significant departure came several years after he gave the Collection to Glasgow, when his concentration on the Ancient Civilisations was an attempt to give it the comprehensiveness desirable for a public gallery. His collecting was never haphazard; Mrs Randolph Hearst said she thought her husband went out and bought things whenever he was worried, but one cannot see Burrell being ruled by his emotions.

The Collection numbers over eight thousand items. Not all are of first rank but even the more journeyman pieces fulfil an essential rôle. The history of artistic endeavour is not written by masterpieces alone: medieval tapestries and sculpture cannot be studied and understood merely from a few great works. By acquiring many pieces within a given field (for example, there are more than seven hundred items of stained glass and nearly fifteen hundred Chinese ceramics) Burrell gave the Collection strength in depth.

The treasures gathered together by many of Burrell's rival collectors have been dispersed; his have not. The Collection is his memorial, as he wished it to be. Burrell refused all suggestions that he should sit for a portrait to be placed in the gallery housing the Collection. The idea was repugnant to him, and in conformity with his wishes there is not even a photograph of him on display there. He used to say:

The collection, not the collector, is the important thing.

The loneliness of the collector: William Randolph Hearst playing patience surrounded by his art treasures at San Simeon. A famous photograph by Dr Salomon (Popperfoto). Many of Burrell's best acquisitions were to come from Hearst's collection.

BURRELL FAMILY PEDIGREE

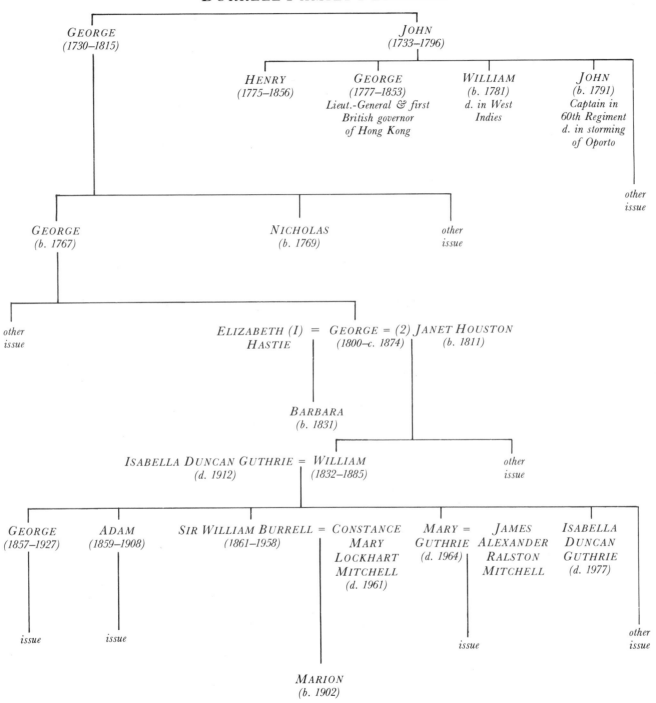

1

BURRELL AND SON

They simply sit and look at him 'making money like slate stones' as he puts it.

Robert Lorimer

SOME time around 1830, if not a few years before, a young Northumbrian named George Burrell made his way north of the border to seek his fortune. The family had been established in Northumberland for several generations and are likely to have been a cadet branch of the Burrells of Broome-park who could trace their ancestry back to an ancient Border family. In the last years of the seventeenth century William Burrell had become the owner of the township of Bassington, in the parish of Eglingham near Alnwick. It was a small estate of some 236 acres with a single farmhouse. In 1770 the brothers George (grandfather of the above-mentioned) and John divided the property between them and soon afterwards sold their moieties separately to the Duke of Northumberland. Two of John's children showed a predilection for a military career. His second son George (1777–1853) rose to the rank of Lieutenant-General and became first British Governor of Hong Kong; John, born in 1791, became a captain in the 60th Regiment of Foot and fell during the storming of Oporto in 1832. Little is known of the other two sons. Henry, the eldest, married the daughter of a Royal Navy captain and died in 1856 at Holbeach in Lincolnshire, and William met his end in the West Indies. Several of the sons and daughters are commemorated by memorials in Long Houghton parish church.

George remained at Bassington as the Duke's tenant and he died there in 1815. His family suffered, as did so many at the time, from an appallingly high infant mortality, no fewer than three daughters dying from smallpox in November and December 1781. Most of the children who survived into adulthood settled in Alnwick, although the second son Nicholas (b. 1769) seems to have moved to Edinburgh, where in 1804 he married Mary Veitch, who came from a Glasgow family. George, the eldest, who was born in 1767, remained in Alnwick where according to one account he was a barge-owner, presumably engaged in coastal trading. Another source says he was a grocer; perhaps he combined the two trades. Both occupations are a far cry from his grandfather's landowning days, albeit on a minor scale, and the fortunes of this branch of the Burrell family had undoubtedly declined. Matters evidently did not improve as the next generation grew up. One son, George (b.1800), followed his father into the barge business, but the prospects locally must have appeared limited and he decided to try his luck in Scotland. In so doing he was to sow the first seeds in the dramatic rise of the family to a level of prosperity it had never known before.

What attracted the young man were the opportunities presented by the Forth & Clyde Canal, which after many delays had been completed in 1790, thereby saving vessels the long and hazardous sea-route around the north coast. Two years later the Monkland Canal was opened, providing convenient passage between the expanding Lanarkshire coalfields and Glasgow; soon after, a junction was formed between the terminus of the Monkland Canal and the Glasgow terminus of the Forth & Clyde at Port Dundas.

Family tradition has it that George Burrell first came north to work on the construction of the Forth & Clyde Canal and although that must be discounted because he had not been born when the Canal was built, it does provide oblique evidence of the importance of this waterway in the commercial history of the Burrells. The Forth & Clyde Canal was from the outset a profitable venture, although in 1802–3 its proprietors short-sightedly rejected the use of steam-ships after the world's first steam-powered vessel, the 'Charlotte Dundas', had navigated the Canal. The cargoes, which comprised the products of Glasgow's rapidly expanding cotton industry, coal, iron, timber, slates and foodstuffs, were transported in vessels with a capacity of about a hundred tons. The Canal also benefited from a demand for passenger traffic. In the early years of the century the Forth & Clyde Navigation Co. introduced a daily passenger service between the eastern and western terminals of Grangemouth and Bowling Bay which proved very popular. By 1836 nearly 200,000 passengers were carried annually on the Canal, compared with a figure of 44,000 for 1812. The income of the proprietors reflected the increasing trade in human and goods traffic. In 1790 it stood at £8,000, by 1795 it had risen to £13,500, in 1798 to £22,000 and in 1814 to £48,071; the dividends paid to shareholders were correspondingly generous.

Profits were still rising when the young George Burrell came to seek his fortune. He is unlikely to have arrived without some prior knowledge of the prospects, for his uncle Nicholas in Edinburgh was in a good position to know how the Canal was faring. Moreover the barges owned by him and his father may have plied their trade as far as Leith. It may indeed have been at the eastern end of the waterway that George established himself initially, for his first child Barbara was born in Leith in 1831. She was his daughter by his marriage to Elizabeth Hastie, who seems to have died giving birth or soon after, for in the same year he married the twenty-year-old Janet Houston, from the village of that name near Bridge of Weir in Renfrewshire. If it was at the eastern terminus that George began he did not remain there long, for by the time his eldest son William had come into the world in 1832 the family had moved to the rapidly expanding city of Glasgow, which is where the story really begins.

Unfortunately George's early career is shrouded in obscurity and one can only surmise what he was doing. Apart from the birthplaces of his two eldest children nothing is known of his movements and activities before the mid-1850's. At the time he arrived in Glasgow it was the third largest city in the United Kingdom, surpassed only by London and Manchester. Its population had doubled in twenty years from 101,000 in 1811 to 202,000 in 1831, and the city was to continue to expand rapidly, with about a million residents (including the suburbs) by the turn of the century. This growth was first stimulated by the textile industry, which in 1831 employed no fewer than 30,600 of a working population of 94,500, and subsequently (between 1830 and 1850) by the development of the iron and coal industries on Clydeside; in the second half of the century the continuing population expansion was prompted by the emergence of the shipbuilding industry on the Clyde, although it had been of no significance when George Burrell came to Glasgow. In spite of these burgeoning industries Glasgow went through cycles of boom and depression; in the second half of the 1820's the city suffered from a slump; the subsequent recovery lasted into the late 1830's, when another recession set in and continued for a decade. These economic fluctuations together with the rapid population increase (largely by immigration from the Highlands and, especially in the 'hungry forties', from Ireland) created grave social problems. A Parliamentary report in 1839 on housing in Great Britain drew attention in no uncertain terms to the overcrowding and foul conditions to be found in the heart of the old city:

> I have seen human degradation in some of the worst places, both in England and abroad, but I did not believe until I had visited the wynds of Glasgow that so large an amount of filth, crime, misery and disease existed in one spot in any civilized country.

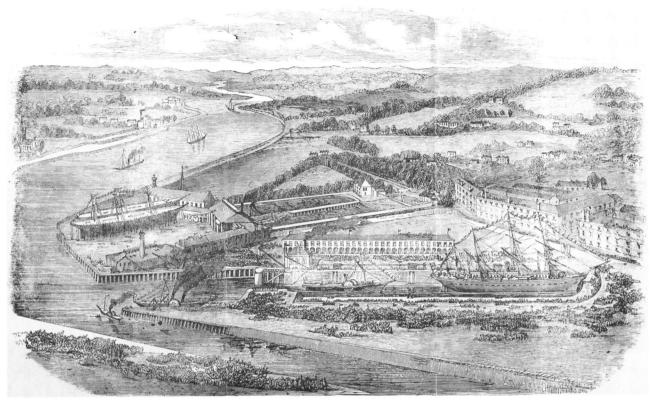

A Clyde shipyard of the 1850's: Tod and McGregor's Yard, Partick, opened in 1858 'with great éclat', according to a contemporary account. (Mitchell Library, Glasgow)

Whatever the problems of the lower echelons of society, there was scope for a man of enterprise and determination to succeed, and the elegant terraces and squares that sprouted to the west in the 1820's and 1830's testify to the prosperity of the expanding middle classes. George Burrell did not yet aspire to such desirable addresses as Blythswood Square; judging from the absence of the family name from the early Post Office Directories it seems that he was working for others for about twenty-five years. The curtain starts to rise with the formation of his own firm in 1856–7.

In the Directory for these years George Burrell is listed as a ship and forwarding agent at the Grangemouth and Alloa Wharf, Port Dundas; in the following year George was joined by his eldest son William and henceforward the firm traded under the name of Burrell and Son. As agents their main concern was arranging the shipment of goods on the Forth & Clyde Canal and for the maintenance of vessels for their owners whilst at Port Dundas. The Glasgow terminus of the Canal was then at the height of its prosperity. A few years earlier a Sunday stroller was amazed at what he observed there:

> On these few acres have been established factories, colour works, chemical works, dye works, grinding works, mills for logwood, dye and bread stuffs, foundries, machine shops, potteries and soap works – presenting a view of manufacturing and curious

industry which must be unparalleled in any other city of the world.

The year in which George Burrell set up business was an important one for all those engaged in traffic on the Canal for it marked the introduction of steam-powered ships. Horse-traction from the banks quickly became obsolete and goods-lighters, luggage-boats and masted lighters were soon driven by screw-propulsion. By 1866 there were no fewer than seventy steam vessels at work on the Forth & Clyde and Monkland Canals. George and William Burrell were no doubt quick to perceive the advantages of steam-power and soon they extended their business into ship-owning. By 1864 at least two vessels were trading in the name of Burrell and Son, the 'Janet Houston', named after the second Mrs George Burrell, and the 'Jeanie Marshall'. These must have been small schooners or smacks with a length determined by the 70-foot locks on the Canal.

The modest beginnings of Burrell and Son in the late 1850's and early 1860's is reflected in the family's unpretentious standard of living. George lived with his wife and family at 72 New City Road, a street of tenements within easy walking distance of Port Dundas and which disappeared in the re-development of the area in the 1960's. They occupied a block which in 1861 housed six families; unlike some of the others the Burrells had no servants. They had five rooms and there were eight in the household – George and Janet Burrell and their six children. The eldest, Barbara, was thirty and the youngest, Alexander was only four (at least three others died in infancy). George, another son, was 22 and his occupation is given as clerk in a shipping agency (presumably Burrell and Son). The eldest son William had recently

The fitting-room of a Glasgow locomotive works, c. 1860. (Mitchell Library, Glasgow)

moved around the corner to 3 Scotia Street, where he occupied three rooms with his wife Isabella (*née* Guthrie) and two infant sons, George and Adam; on 9 July of that year their numbers were augmented by the birth of a third son, William. The trades of the other residents of 3 Scotia Street give a good indication of the social status of the Burrells at this time. They comprised a mixture of artisan and lower middle-class occupations, including dress-maker, upholsterer, grocer, draper, schoolmaster and mill merchant.

Although the Forth & Clyde Canal remained a busy waterway, by the middle decades of the century it faced serious competition from the railways. The Glasgow–Edinburgh line opened in 1842 and as much of the route ran parallel with the Forth & Clyde it very quickly attracted the passenger traffic away from the Canal. A tariff war developed with this and other railway companies for the goods and minerals traffic in which inevitably the Canal was the loser. The decline in revenue was accelerated by the gradual exhaustion of the colleries near the banks of the Canal. In 1867, in order to obtain the port of Grangemouth, which was owned by the Forth & Clyde Navigation Company, for the dispatch of Lanarkshire coal to the Continent, the Caledonian Railway Company was forced to purchase the Canal as well. Notwithstanding the expenditure of large sums on dredging and maintenance by the Caledonian, traffic continued to decrease: between 1868 and 1888 tonnage carried fell from 3,022,583 to 1,257,206 and revenue from £87,145 to £44,038.

George Burrell and his son quite soon saw the writing on the wall and although the Canal trade remained sufficiently profitable for them

1 VIRGIN AND CHILD by Giovanni Bellini (c. 1430–1516), the first of the great Venetian painters of the Renaissance.

2 One of the prize Chinese bronzes in the Collection – a 'steamer' of the late Shang or early Zhou dynasty (11th century BC).

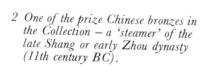

3 *Details from the GRAPE HARVEST
(see page 24).*

never to abandon it, they realised the need to spread their interests. In 1866, perhaps with foreknowledge of the imminent takeover of the Canal, they formed a partnership with Thomas McLaren as ship and insurance brokers and agents, chiefly concerned with the sale and purchase of vessels. In the 1871 Post Office Directory they are described as agents for steamers to Spain, Portugal and the Mediterranean, and China via the Suez Canal. The offices of the partnership were initially in St Vincent Street, later transferred to 141 Buchanan Street. Simultaneously the Burrells ventured into deep-sea shipowning with the ordering from Swan's yard of the 'Fitzwilliam', an iron steamer. The 'Fitzwilliam' was destined for trading around the coasts of the British Isles and the near Continent. In 1868 she was joined by the 'Fitzjames', of 520 gross tons, which was built to operate in a similar area, although later her range was extended to the Mediterranean. The third addition to this embryonic fleet was a much larger vessel than the other two and shows the abilities of Burrell *père* and *fils* to perceive commercial advantages quickly. The 'Strathclyde', which was built by Blackwood and Gordon at Port Glasgow and launched in January 1871, was of 1,951 gross tons and was designed for the India trade. The Burrells had seen almost at once the enormous benefits from trade with the Far East to be gained from the Suez Canal, which had opened shortly before the 'Strathclyde' was laid down. Another difference was that this vessel did not operate under the house flag of Burrell and Son, but seems to have been a speculative venture and was chartered to Gellatly, Hankey, Sewell and Company. This was not a novel practice for Scottish ship-owners: in the 1850's, for example, the Thomsons of Leith frequently chartered their ships.

The 'Strathclyde' is also significant as the first of many Burrell ships to bear the 'Strath' prefix. In adopting a prefix which virtually became a trademark the Burrells contributed to the growth of a fashion amongst ship-owners. In 1853 the Thomsons ordered the first in a series of what was to become the 'Ben' Line, and Cayzer, Irvine & Company of Liverpool and Glasgow and Hugh Hogarth soon followed on the heels of Burrell and Son with their respective 'Clans' and 'Barons'. When in the early 1930's the P. and O. Line used the 'Strath' prefix for five new liners Sir William Burrell was rather annoyed at not being consulted.

In conformity with long-established custom in the shipping world shares in each of the Burrell ships were reckoned as 64 of $1/64$ each, with the profits (or losses) on the voyages distributed on a pro rata basis. The system also enabled the prospective ship-owner to raise the capital to build or buy his vessel and operate it. The Burrells held half the shares in each of the first three ships, the other 32 being in the name of A.C. Wotherspoon (the 'Fitzwilliam') and their shipbroking partner Thomas McLaren (the 'Fitzjames' and the 'Strathclyde'). The Burrell shares were in William's name, not his father's, and it is probable that the venture into ocean-going ships, which were engaged in tramping and not liner trades, was on his initiative.

In these early years small holdings were held by the Burrells in a number of other vessels, including the wooden barque 'Suffolk' and the steamer 'Galata'. Another, the steamer 'Grange', was also managed by them from 1869 until her loss in the Loire estuary four years later. The managing of ships in which they were only minor shareholders or had no financial interest at all was probably the most important aspect of the Burrells' activities during the late 1870's and 1880's. Their rôle as such was to maintain the ship whilst in port, arranging for supplies, fuel, cargo handling, payment of charges and insurance, and not least, selecting crews. What remuneration Burrell and Son received for its labours has not been established; probably the firm was on a set fee: around 1850 William Thomson of Alloa's fee was £20 per vessel.

By 1875 Burrell and Son's fleet had expanded and comprised six steamers, most of which carried cargoes to and from the Mediterranean, but with the 'Strathclyde' still engaged on the Indian route; at 2,436 gross tons the newly-built 'Strathleven' was the largest ship, and was designed to carry the firm's flag even further afield, to Australia and China.

A random glance at the 'Clyde Bills of Entry and Shipping List' for February and March 1875 reveals details of cargoes, trade routes and the volume of business. On 26 February the 'Fitzclarence', in which Burrell and Son had a major stake, arrived at Glasgow with a crew of eighteen under a master named Houston (a relative of George Burrell's second wife?). The cargo consisted of 895 tons of sulphur ore taken on at Huelva and corkwood, wine, seed oil and oranges from Lisbon. Three weeks later, laden with 800 tons of coal valued at £480, she sailed for Gibraltar. In the same two months Burrell and Son is named as agents

for three ships entering and leaving Glasgow, all of which were engaged on the Huelva–Lisbon route.

In October 1877 the firm attracted national publicity in unexpected fashion. One of its ships, the 'Fitzmaurice', en route from Middlesbrough to Valencia with a cargo of pig iron, sighted a vessel carrying the famous obelisk known as Cleopatra's Needle from Alexandria to London drifting abandoned in the Bay of Biscay. The crew of the 'Fitzmaurice' secured it and towed it to Ferrol, for which feat a salvage award of £2,000 was subsequently made to Burrell and Son. In a perhaps uncharacteristic gesture William Burrell offered to forego the award if the Needle was erected at Greenock.

By this date William was in sole charge, his father having died a few years before. He almost immediately began to expand the business. The ship-broking partnership with Thomas McLaren, which had been dissolved in 1872, was replaced by another in the name of Burrell and Son at the same address, and a new shipping agency, Burrell and Haig, was formed with its offices at Port Dundas. He also ventured into shipbuilding with the establishment of a yard at Hamiltonhill, by Port Dundas. It may have existed before just for the maintenance of the Burrell vessels using the Forth & Clyde Canal, and the irregular production of new craft throughout its history suggests that repair and maintenance was always the yard's primary function. Nonetheless the new vessels launched there represented quite an important string to the family's commercial bow. The craft conformed to a specific type,

*The 'Ashdale Glen', 70 tons gross,
off Ardlamont in 1926.
She was broken up in about 1933.
(Dan McDonald)*

known widely and affectionately as the 'Clyde Puffer'. This was a small but sturdy steamer which was first developed in the 1850's to carry goods on the Canal and off-load using its own gear. The size of the locks did not permit a length greater than 66 feet and its cargo capacity was a hundred tons. During the 1860's and 1870's two variants evolved, one for estuary work and the second an 'outside' or sea-going boat, engaged in coastal and island trade. These capable and reliable craft had a long career, only disappearing from Scottish waters about twenty years ago. Altogether some four hundred puffers were built, and of the several yards specialising in their production, that at Hamiltonhill owned by the Burrells had the third highest total, following Swan's and J. & J. HKAS. Between 1875 and its closure in 1903 at least fifty puffers were launched in the Hamiltonhill yard. Some were built for the firm's own use, such as the 'Terrier' (1884). A considerable number were constructed for sale to other owners, like the 'Ashdale Glen' (1893) and the 'Dorothy' (1901). The latter is described in a recent book on these vessels as a typical example from the Burrell shipyard, very tidy and a good carrier.

The Hamiltonhill yard was registered in the name of Burrell and *Sons* and it is almost certain that it was there that William's eldest son George began to acquire his technical knowledge, probably about the time that building of puffers began. George was then eighteen years old; he was very soon to be joined in the family business by his brother William, a mere stripling of fourteen.

Details of the early years and upbringing of the future Sir William Burrell are lacking. His mother by all accounts was a strong, even stern, personality, an impression which finds confirmation in her portrait by

The young Burrells: left to right, William, George, Adam.

Burrell's favourite sister Mary, painted by Sir John Lavery in 1895. See also pages 71 and 72.

Henry. William was devoted to her. Judging from his adult habits the young boy seems to have had a strict and formal upbringing with few (if any) luxuries. The family was large: in addition to the three eldest boys, George, Adam and William, who appear together in a photograph taken before any of them attained adolescence, there was another brother, Henry, and five sisters, at least one of whom died in childhood. All four brothers were at one time or another to be associated with the family business, although only George and William were to stay the course. Henry became an accountant and Adam, who was the least conformist, left the firm after a while to study medicine at Glasgow. This move seems to have aroused the strong disapproval of the commercially-minded Burrell family and on qualifying Adam and his Irish wife and children emigrated to the United States and thence soon after to South Africa before finally settling in New Zealand, where he died in 1908. He was reputedly a clever man but possessed of an awesome temper which was quickly aroused. Little can be said of the girls, with the exception of Mary, the youngest. She appears to have been William's favourite sister and grew up to be a most attractive young woman, inheriting her mother's bright blue eyes, as Lavery's portrait reveals. She was described in her twenties by William's best friend the rising Scottish architect Robert Lorimer (1864–1929) as pleasant and intelligent, although he was put off as a suitor by her Glasgow accent!

The first years of William Burrell's life were spent in a number of homes. In 1862 the family moved from Scotia Street to 30 Willowbank Street, a modest tenement building off Woodlands Road in the West End of the city. Ten years later they were settled outside the city limits at Bowling; they were still there a few years later after the death of William Burrell senior in 1885.

The young William was away for lengthy periods from Bowling at boarding school in St Andrews. This is likely to have been Abbey Park, a prestigious preparatory school which around 1870 had about seventy boarders. The imposing ruins of the Cathedral and Archbishop's palace together with the splendid castles of the Fife peninsula may well have left an impression on the boy's subconscious, and been the basis of his great love for medieval art, but at the time it is doubtful if they attracted more than his passing glance. It was, however, in his school-days that his interest in art was actively aroused, albeit in a later period than the middle ages.

There are several different tales about his juvenile ventures into the art world. According to one version an unrecognised picture by Raeburn was knocked down to him at a Glasgow auction for a small sum; the young schoolboy asked his father for a contribution, pointing out the bargain he was getting. William Burrell, however, whose sharp business brain did not extend to the rarified world of connoisseurship, was unimpressed and not only refused to give the boy any money but lectured him on his extravagance. The young lad had no option but to put the picture back into the saleroom, where it failed to reach the amount he had paid and so he lost on the exercise. A variant of the story has Burrell at the age of eighteen buying a Romney portrait for about £10. This is the more likely of the two tales, but as there are no longer any paintings in the Collection by either artist which are known to have been acquired in his early years of collecting, neither version can be

verified. They do at least agree that it was eighteenth-century British portraiture which appealed to the young Burrell.

    The truth of the matter is that nothing of significance emerged from these early purchases; in later years Burrell used to say that their chief value lay in the frames and there are no grounds for challenging this assertion from the one person who was in a position to know. Quite possibly he burned his fingers on a few occasions and these early experiences may underlie his later careful selection of dealers.

    Precisely what sparked off this interest in art at a very early age is not certain. In his obituary of Burrell in the Scotsman, Andrew Hannah, Depute Director of Glasgow Museums and Art Galleries, said:

> He told me that it was from his mother that he derived interest in the Arts. She fired him with ambition not only to get to know the fundamentals of great art, but to set about acquiring many of the finest specimens procurable.

This statement is supported by some members of the family, although others and various close friends deny that his mother had any such

Mother and son out for a drive in the country: Mrs Burrell and William. The photograph was probably taken in the 1890's. (Alan Mitchell)

influence. She seems at least to have had some artistic leanings, for as we shall see, she accompanied Burrell on several of his expeditions abroad. Of one thing we can be sure: his aesthetic tastes received no encouragement from his father. The latter's attitude as outlined in the tale of the Raeburn has the ring of truth, and it is also said that on another occasion the young William annoyed him by spending his pocket-money on a painting rather than a cricket bat! In one sense William Burrell senior did affect very deeply his son's collecting interests, albeit unknowingly. Burrell's dealings with the art world always reflected very closely his business upbringing. The commercial habits and instincts inculcated into him from his early days with the family firm never left him. He retained to the end a determination to get the best at the lowest price and always had more faith in the man of business rather than scholars and academics. Perhaps if he had left home and gone to university his attitude would have been different. The evidence of his library and correspondence suggests that he was never a great reader on art; he relied rather on his eye and judgement. In this he was unlike many other self-made collectors who depended over-much on their cheque-books and the advice of others.

This was to emerge in the future. All that can be said for certain is that Burrell very early on developed a taste for art. The opportunities to indulge it were in any case very limited for at fourteen he was whisked away from school and put into the family business.

As William Burrell later recounted, his entry into the firm in 1875 occurred somewhat unexpectedly. Just before he was due to return to school after the holidays his father took him into the Buchanan Street offices and went off to attend to some business. He returned to find his son helping the ledger clerks with such a grasp of the work that he told him there was no point in sending him back to school. And so the young William began work at a clerk's salary.

For the next ten years he and George learned the business under their father's shrewd direction. Their responsibilities were divided. George, who was probably first at the Hamiltonhill yard, later went to a larger shipbuilding concern at Dumbarton to obtain a firm grasp of technical developments. His brother William was assigned to the commercial and financial side. As he grew to maturity this involved him in frequent travels abroad to foster and maintain the firm's commercial contracts. His journeys were mainly confined to Europe, particularly Vienna, but in his twenties he went further afield to Australia and New Zealand. He used these travels to inform himself on the visual arts, compensating for his lack of formal education.

During these years Burrell and Son continued to expand and prosper. In 1880–1 it moved into more prestigious premises at 54 George Square, where it remained until 1928–9. The firm stayed sufficiently modest in size to avoid the cut-throat competition that developed between the large liner-shipping companies, particularly in the 1880's when freight rates were very depressed. It was in this period that the Clyde shipyards obtained a great share of the market thanks to the growth of steelworks in the area and the pioneering of innovations in marine engineering. These included new boiler designs to cope with higher steam pressures and firstly compound and then triple expansion engines which achieved much-desired economy in fuel consumption on the long-haul routes. Although subject to violent depressions as well as boom years, shipbuilding on the Clyde in the late 1870's outstripped all other British centres and tonnage rose dramatically from just under 200,000 in 1876 to more than 400,000 in 1882. In the former year one-third of all British tonnage was built on the Clyde and its shipyards were to retain their supremacy until the great depression of the 1930's.

Most of the ships built for Burrell and Son in this decade came from local yards, chiefly that of Blackwood and Gordon at Port Glasgow. The firm was not slow to take advantage of technical advances, as is shown by the ordering of a steel-hulled vessel, the 'Adria', only a year or so after William Denny and Brothers of Dumbarton had launched the first ocean-going ship so constructed in 1878.

For a brief period the Burrells themselves went in for large-scale shipbuilding. In so doing they were making a virtue out of necessity. In January 1881 an order for two steam-ships priced at about £18,000 each was placed by Burrell and Son with Robert Chambers junior of Lower Woodyard, Dumbarton. Soon after he went bankrupt and in order to cut their losses and ensure delivery the elder William Burrell took over the yard. For a ship-owner to make such a move was not without precedent: in 1873 the Anchor Line had become co-owners of Tod and McGregor's yard at Partick. It is probable that George Burrell was closely concerned with Lower Woodyard. During the three years in which they ran the yard at least fourteen sea-going vessels, ranging in size from 376 to 2,252 gross tons, and six barges were launched there. Rather surprisingly only a few of the ships went into service with Burrell and Son as sole owners or major shareholders; the majority were constructed for other firms, such as James Hay and Sons ('Strath-nairn' and 'Strathness') and a Genoese company, Navigazione Generale Italiano ('Bormida' and 'Bisagno').

The two ships that were on the stocks when Chambers went bankrupt did not join Burrell and Son's fleet on completion, but instead went to the Adria Hungarian Sea Navigation Company; over the next three years Burrell and Son sold several of their own vessels to the same company. The origins of this connection lay in the desire by the Hungarian government to encourage services to and from its Adriatic coast, which then included parts of what is now Jugoslavia. Burrell and

Son obtained one of these contracts, to run a regular steamer service between the principal port of Fiume (now Rijeka), Glasgow and Leith. In 1879, together with Schenker and Co. of Vienna, Budapest and Fiume, Burrell and Son formed the Adria Steamship Company to ply this route. The following year it was sold to the Hungarian government which re-formed it as the Adria Hungarian Sea Navigation Company, for which Burrell and Son remained general agents until the First World War. This Austro-Hungarian link was particularly important for Burrell and Son in the 1880's and 1890's, and between 1879 and 1883 a series of vessels averaging 1,200 gross tons were built specifically for this Adriatic trade route. They were given Hungarian names, such as the 'Tisza' and the 'B. Kemeny', named respectively after the Hungarian premier and Minister of Finance. Several were designed specifically for Hungarian cargoes like flour and wood. Between the Burrells and Gottfried Schenker there was a long-standing family friendship which was of considerable commercial importance. The Schenker connection is an early indication of what was to be a crucial Burrell policy, to rely on far-flung contacts for obtaining cargoes rather than on the masters of their ships.

William Burrell senior did not neglect his other routes. The larger ships, those with the 'Strath' prefix, continued to ply between the Clyde and the Far East. The 'Strathclyde' sank in the English Channel in 1876 with the loss of 38 lives, but she was replaced six years later by the 'Strathmore', the first second-hand ship purchased by Burrell and Son. The 'Strathleven' achieved fame in February 1880 when under charter to a group of Australian businessmen she became the first ship to carry a cargo of refrigerated meat from Australia to Great Britain. It is a little surprising that Burrell and Son apparently failed to perceive the significance of this event and they did not enter the meat-shipping trade which was to have such an important effect on the economies of Australia and New Zealand.

Burrell ships were also to be seen in the western hemisphere. In 1880 the firm became the Glasgow agents for Joseph Hoult's line of steamers operating from Liverpool to the West Indies. Four years later Burrell and Son ordered their own vessel for this trade, appropriately named the 'Rio Bueno'. At 1,706 gross tons she was larger than the rest of the fleet with the exception of the 'Straths'.

While the destinies of Burrell and Son were in the hands of William Burrell senior the firm thus diversified its interests extensively. In addition to its agencies and managerial functions, which always seem to have been of major importance although they have attracted less attention, it had ventured (albeit briefly) into large-scale shipbuilding and had opened up new routes. With the 'Straths' plying the routes to the Far East, the 'Rio Bueno' to the West Indies, the 'Fitzes' busy on the Mediterranean and Baltic runs and the 'Hungarian' vessels carrying cargoes between Glasgow and Fiume, there were few corners of the globe where the Burrell house flag (a blue swallowtail with a red cross formé within a white circle) was not to be seen. In spite of this expansion the family retained a tight control. Of the 27 ships built for Burrell and Son in 1864–85 the entire shareholdings in nine were in the name of William Burrell; sole ownership on such a scale was very unusual. Even those ships where the shares were distributed among several individuals were sold on the strict proviso that the vessels remained under the management and flag of Burrell and Son. As managing owner William Burrell was in a happy position. In addition to any profit (or loss) he made on each voyage as a shareholder he would take a fixed fee or percentage of gross earnings as a management charge (in the case of Cayzer, Irvine and Company the rate was $2\frac{1}{2}\%$). The writer of *Clydeside Cameos* summarised the situation of a managing owner:

> A managing owner . . . charges his commission on the gross earnings of the vessel, and it really does not matter a brass farthing to him whether the net result be profit or loss.

Some managing owners also negotiated contracts which gave them a commission on the net profits as well as the gross earnings of the vessel. Charles Cayzer took 5%, but it has not been established whether William Burrell did likewise.

By the middle of the 1880's matters were undoubtedly going well for the Burrell family. The firm was expanding quietly and unspectacularly and the sons were learning the business while growing to maturity. William Burrell may well have intended their apprenticeship to be a lengthy one. If so it was not to be, for on 21 June 1885 he died at the comparatively young age of 53. This left the two sons, aged 28 and 24, at the helm and there must have been more than a few in Glasgow shipping circles who wondered at their ability to survive the cut-throat competition and volatile markets. The brothers were soon to give their answer in no uncertain terms. Under their daring but shrewd direction Burrell and Son underwent a dramatic transformation; in so doing the two young men made fortunes.

The two brothers divided their responsibilities according to their respective training and experience. George handled the technical specifications of new ships and oversaw their construction, whilst William managed the commercial and financial side. The latter had grown into a tall and slender young man, of upright stance and with a small moustache. He spoke with a pronounced Scottish burr and a nasal twang, and although he had a keen if dry sense of humour (which he was to retain all his life) he did not spare either himself or his employees. James Rough, who joined Burrell and Son as an office boy in 1907, recalled that 'he was very demanding that everything be done perfectly and in order. He demanded efficiency from everybody and everybody gave it.' Rough also singled out Burrell's 'stern and thorough manner of training, and his delegation of responsibility'. This *penchant* for detail and precision was equally applied in later years to the recording of his art collection.

For the first three years after their father's death William and George made no startling changes, being content to let things tick over while they found their feet. On the domestic front George, who celebrated the birth of his first child in the same year as his father died, was living at Langbank and William, still unmarried, remained in the family home at Bowling with his mother and other brothers and sisters. Two of the girls were sent abroad to complete their education, as is evidenced by the two earliest letters written by William Burrell which have come to light. They provide valuable insight into family life and business activities, as well as his personality. They were both addressed to his teenaged sister Isabella ('Bella'), who was staying with a family in Paris. The first is dated 26 January 1890 and contains the following passage:

> We are all well at home – but Mother frets a little when she does not get your letter within the week. . . . I always tell her it will come next morning but I think if you could arrange to write her on the same day every week (putting it down in your diary) it would be better. For the rest of us it doesn't matter so much but to Mother it makes a great difference as she feels your and Mary's absence very much and if she doesn't hear from you regularly begins to think there is something wrong. I sent you the two drafts on the 10th, one for £14 and the other for £1 and am glad you got them allright. I meant to write you that day but hadn't a moment to do so, so thought it better to send you the money so I did rather than be a day late with Madame Monod.
> . . . . Mary wrote me recently that a youth at Lausanne had sent her his card and a box of sweets and that she very properly immediately returned both. I consider this was worse than cheeky on his part and am glad she had the good sense to snub him as she did. Characters like that abound everywhere and it behoves every young girl to be on her guard. I can only hope that God will preserve you both from all such. When you are away from your Mothers care you cannot be too careful yourself. George is getting on but still slowly and I dont know when he will be back to the office. I hope this will find you very well and with love from all.
> > Believe me Dear Bella
> > > Your loving brother
> > > W. Burrell

Had one not known otherwise, the tone of this letter would lead one to believe that it was written by a man in his middle age, rather than a 28 year-old. In his care for his sister's moral welfare Burrell is prim, almost priggish. He harped on the same theme in the second letter, written on 2 March in the same year:

I hope Bella that you are keeping well and being well guided, for in a city like Paris a young girl cannot be too careful. Your Mother is often very anxious about you and is very nervous and really ill when your letter does not arrive punctually . . . so I beg of you as you value your Mother to spare her any trouble of this sort. It is, I think the least we can all do. I hope you are getting on with your studies well. I am sure you are. We are all keeping well at home, everything is moving along much the same as usual. With much love Believe me
    Dear Bella,
        Your affect Brother
            W. Burrell

His moralising attitude, however, is entirely typical of a strictly brought-up Victorian middle class head of the family, which was the rôle William Burrell had to fill since his father's death and his eldest brother's marriage. Indeed in both letters he sounds far more like a father than a brother. The impression given is that the family was very close-knit and there can be no doubt of Burrell's affection for his mother and sister. In the references in the first letter to the payments to Madame Monod there is apparent a keenness for prompt payment, an admirable practice and one to which he adhered throughout his life.

At the time these letters were written Burrell and Son was undergoing a dramatic transformation, which startled the shipping world. Between them George and William possessed the ideal qualities of a managing owner as defined by A.W. Kirkcaldy in his *British Shipping*, published in 1914:

> The first great qualification required . . . is a knowledge of men, an unerring judgement. . . . He must be ever on the alert to note new developments connected both with the type of ship he is employing, and with all the conditions and circumstances of the trade in which he is taking part.

These attributes were well to the fore when in 1888–90 no fewer than ten new ships were built for Burrell and Son, which set it on the road to becoming one of the largest steam-ship companies based in Glasgow. These vessels were chiefly designed to expand the long-haul fleet, which at that time consisted only of the 'Strathmore' and the 'Strathleven'. They were employed on the routes to India, China and Japan, on liner services, on charter to other companies and in tramping.

This dramatic expansion of the fleet kept William extremely busy, and his burden must have been considerably increased by George's absence through illness in a critical period. This illness, or more accurately, his convalescence, is mentioned in William's first letter to Isabella, quoted above. The same letter also includes some interesting remarks on his shipping affairs:

> We have had another launch since I last wrote you:– She was named the 'Strathdon' and is a sister ship to the 'Strathdee'. No

One of the 1888–90 fleet: SS 'Strathavon', built by Russell and Company of Greenock and launched in June 1890. (Museum of Transport, Glasgow)

one was present but Mr Stewart our Superintendent and the builders wife. She broke the bottle and altogether for a 4000 tonner the ceremony could not have been of a less imposing nature. Unless those interested rush to make an occasion of it I think the quieter it is done the better. I am afraid we have also lost a steamer the 'Strathblane'. She went ashore at the Cape of Good Hope last week with a most valuable cargo and is not expected to get off.

The 'Strathdon' was built by the Tyne Iron Shipbuilding Company and the 'Strathblane' was also one of the new orders and had only been delivered in 1888. Burrell's fears regarding the latter were justified and she was a total loss. The subsequent enquiry found that the Pilot was at least partly to blame.

Rather more of the flavour of William Burrell's hectic commercial life at this time is conveyed in the letter of 2 March (which also furnishes the personal detail that he was prone to sea-sickness):

I got your kind letter allright and would have written to you sooner but I have been exceedingly busy. Last Sunday I had to go up to London and the Sunday before to Newcastle to attend the trial trip of the 'Strathdon' our last Tyne steamer. It (Monday) was a most miserable day and I was wretchedly sick, worse than on the way out to Australia or on the way home. The 'Strathdon' is loading at London for the Cape of Good Hope. Last Saturday ie 22nd Feby the 'Strathesk' was launched and we had a very pleasant little meeting. Miss McKaig [presumably a relative of George Burrell's wife] broke the bottle. Mother was down and so was Mr Henry Birkmyre with his two youngest daughters and I think they all rather enjoyed the outing.

All of the new ships bore the 'Strath' prefix. They ranged in gross tonnage from 2,271 to 3,265, and seven of them were sister-ships, with almost identical details and dimensions. Their technical specifications were very different from the earlier ships built for Burrell and Son – George Burrell was well aware of new advances. All were built of steel (with the exception of the 'Adria' all the earlier vessels had been iron-hulled) and their engine-rooms contained boilers capable of 160 lb per square inch pressures compared with the 60–90 lb achieved by the older ships in the fleet; moreover they were powered by triple-expansion engines which were much more economical than the compound engines fitted previously. The new ships had steam-powered deck machinery and other fittings which ensured that they were included on the Admiralty list as suitable for transport in wartime. Finally a number contained accommodation for a small number of

4 Devonshire Gardens, Glasgow, Burrell's home in the 1890's as it is today.

first-class passengers. At the same time as these ships were being constructed the Burrells fitted five of their existing fleet with the new boilers and triple-expansion engines. The figures for the 'Strathleven' reveal a remarkable improvement in efficiency. She was now capable of $10\frac{3}{4}$ knots on 17 tons of coal per day compared with the $9\frac{3}{4}$ knots on 23 tons achieved with her original boilers and compound engines.

Although three of the new steamers (the 'Strathearn', 'Strathblane' and 'Stratheadrick') were lost within two years of launching, the others brought handsome profits to their managing owners and shareholders, handsome enough for William in 1891–2 to buy a large new house at 4 Devonshire Gardens along the prestigious Great Western Road. In the distribution of shares there is a considerable change from their father's day. To finance the construction of so many new and large ships was beyond the resources of William and George, and sole ownership of all 64 shares in each ship was out of the question. Their reputation was sufficiently high for them to have no difficulty in selling the shares. Some were held by members of the family, like their mother, others by business associates in Glasgow and elsewhere in Britain. The only foreign shareholder was their old friend Gottfried Schenker, with whom Burrell and Son in 1895 formed the Austro-Hungarian Steamship Company to operate a cargo service between the Adriatic and the United States. The route was served by eleven second-hand iron compound steamers in the six years of the firm's existence. Through Schenker the Burrells retained close links with the Austro-Hungarian Empire and from 1888 William was its Vice-Consul in Glasgow. After the dissolution of the Empire he became Consul for Hungary and George filled the corresponding post for Austria. The award of the Iron Cross class III to William was proposed at one time, but it foundered on the fact that he was not a citizen of the Empire.

Schenker's name and the absence of the masters of the firm's ships from the lists of shareholders show how much the Burrells relied on overseas agents for business. In some companies it was the practice to encourage the master to take at least one share in his ship as an incentive to obtain cargoes; in common with Cayzer, Irvine and Company's Clan Line, the Burrells preferred to use their masters merely as paid employees and placed the responsibility for negotiating freight in the hands of appointed agents such as Gottfried Schenker. It was a particularly important function in tramping, as it was essential to avoid passages in ballast between cargoes. William Burrell was always careful to nurture and keep an eye on his agents. Robert Lorimer noted that he travelled all over Europe two or three times a year on visits to the firm's agents.

Lorimer and Burrell first met in the autumn of 1897 at Earlshall, the Fife home of R.W. MacKenzie, a collector of tapestries and furniture.

They were both bachelors in their thirties and of similar temperament. This in the long run was to prove a disastrous handicap to their friendship, but on first acquaintance the two men found much in common. Lorimer's closest friend at the time was R.S. Dods, an Australian architect who had served his apprenticeship in Edinburgh with him. Dods had returned to his native country and Lorimer's letters to him are the primary source of information on Burrell in the years around the turn of the century. The first in which he is mentioned is dated 12 February 1898 and reveals that Burrell was by this time an art collector of some standing:

> I don't think I told you of my Glasgow client. A young Glasgow shipowner named Burrell, he came to Earlshall with his sisters in autumn and Mac[Kenzie] saw him. He's dying to get hold of an old castle, and would turn me loose on one tomorrow if I could find one for him but I can't, but he's a rare good chap to be with and I'll land him in for something yet. He travels pretty well all over Europe 2–3 times a year, visiting their agents, and is a great buyer of furniture, etc., and really has very fine taste (God knows where he got it and his knowledge from). I went through to spend a night with them a few weeks ago, lives with his mother and 2 rather engaging sisters. He's 36: he possesses 17 Matthew Maris's – 2 Whistlers and God knows what else, and really a lot of beautiful old furniture and brass. Finest lot of these deep brass dishes I ever saw.

A letter written in January 1902 provides valuable insight also into Burrell's business acumen:

> His scheme is really the nimblest I've ever struck. He sells his fleet when there is the periodical boom and then puts his money into 3 per c[ent] stock and lies back until things are absolutely in the

Two 16th-century brass dishes of the very kind referred to by Lorimer in his first letter to Dods.

gutter – soup kitchen times – everyone starving for a job. He then goes like a roaring lion. Orders a dozen large steamers in a week, gets them built at rock bottom prices, less than $\frac{1}{2}$ what they'd have cost him last year. Then by the time they're delivered to him things have begun to improve a little bit and there he is ready with a tip top fleet of brand new steamers and owing to the cheap rate he's had them built at, ready to carry cheaper than anybody. Sounds like a game anyone could play at but none of them have the pluck to do it. They simply sit and look at him 'making money like slate stones' as he expresses it.

Lorimer's account can be verified from Lloyd's Register. Within the space of a few weeks at the end of 1893 Burrell and Son prepared to augment its fleet by asking for tenders for no fewer than twelve large steam-ships from yards on the Clyde and Tyne, all of which were delivered in 1894. At the time the shipping industry was in a very depressed state. The slump was at its worst in the year the Burrells placed their orders; consequently they were able to have the ships built at a very economical cost, ranging between £39,000 and £43,500. The depression also affected the price of second-hand vessels, and taking advantage of this the brothers bought nine ships in 1893–4. The second-hand ships were iron-built with compound engines, but the new steamers were very up-to-date. The twelve new 'Straths' were the largest to join the fleet to date, averaging four thousand gross tons, and including the 'Strathgyle', which at 5,023 gross tons was the biggest vessel ever to carry the flag of Burrell and Son. They had telescopic masts to enable them to navigate the Manchester Ship Canal and the boilers were fitted with Howden's patent forced draught which supplied a triple-expansion engine giving a speed of about twelve knots. They were designed for world-wide tramping, carrying freight to and from the United States, West Indies, India and the Far East and Australia. To order a dozen steamers at a time when other companies were cutting back in an over-loaded market demanded enormous nerve and self-confidence, but the brothers' reading of the situation was proved correct, to their own benefit and that of their shareholders. Soon after the new ships joined the fleet the slump began to bottom out, and as Lorimer observed, because they had been built so cheaply, Burrell and Son was able to attract more freight business by undercutting competitors.

William in particular was famed for his boldness and opportunism. On one occasion he learned that the Royal Navy was sending a squadron to show the British flag in a distant part of the globe. Ascertaining the fuel consumption and bunker capacity of the ships concerned, William calculated that they would run short of fuel, and dispatched several of his fleet loaded with coal to one of the squadron's ports of call. The resulting profit was handsome.

William and George Burrell undoubtedly had the Midas touch. In 1898–1900, having enjoyed several years of profitable trading from the new ships and many years from the older vessels, they decided to take advantage of the current high prices obtainable for shipping and sold the entire fleet. Moreover in 1901 the last recorded puffer was launched in the Hamiltonhill yard and it finally closed two years later. The proceeds were distributed amongst all the shareholders and with his money invested (if Lorimer is correct) in 3% stock William went into semi-retirement for a while, although the firm continued to act as agents and brokers. He was not yet forty and had already made a fortune.

For the next few years he found much to occupy his mind in civic matters. In 1899 he was elected to the Council of Glasgow Corporation as one of the representatives for the Exchange Ward and became convenor of a sub-committee on health. The journal the Bailie in its issue of 5 November 1902 describes Burrell's work in this field:

> On the subject of the hour, the great housing problems, his views are clear and defined. While they are in no sense narrow or hidebound, they show lucid but entirely sympathetic insight and appreciation of the many difficulties and possible dangers surrounding what is the most complex and pressing of current municipal questions.

Burrell aged 39.
From an illustration in the Bailie,
5 November 1902.

The Bailie was an official organ and therefore was inclined to write in eulogistic terms about the elected representatives. It is apparent from the Lorimer–Dods correspondence that Burrell's active interest in political and social affairs was never intended to be more than temporary, filling a slack period of business. Nonetheless there is no reason to doubt that the appalling housing problems of Glasgow troubled his conscience and that he applied his energy and business experience wholeheartedly into attempting to alleviate the situation. He was particularly concerned with re-housing the inhabitants of some of the worst slums, but discovered as have others in more recent times, that they sometimes preferred to stay as they were in familiar surroundings. On one occasion he had a brick aimed at him.

Burrell also played his part in other public affairs during the opening years of the century. From 1903 until 1905 he served as a magistrate and he was one of the most active members of the Committee for the art section of the Glasgow International Exhibition of 1901. At the same time he was pursuing his interests in collecting.

These years also saw important changes in Burrell's private life. In September 1898 Lorimer had joined a Burrell family party on holiday in the Netherlands. The group included another friend of William Burrell named James Alexander Ralston Mitchell, who was a member of the family which owned the shipping firm of Edminston and

Mitchell. Marital alliances were common in the close-knit mercantile community of late Victorian Glasgow and sure enough two years later Mitchell and Mary Burrell became engaged. This happened on another family holiday in Germany. Lorimer commented: 'The moonlight at Rothenburg proved too much for them.' When they married in 1901 William's presents were very generous and included a diamond necklet, a mother-of-pearl fan and silver dishes.

In the same year William Burrell at the age of 39 further cemented the Mitchell connection by announcing his engagement to Ralston's sister Constance. Lorimer gave his reactions to Dods:

> Wants me to be his best man. I'm awfully pleased about it. He's rolling in money and 38 [sic] so it's time he was spliced and she is an extremely pretty, most refined looking girl, with a quite angelic temper.

A few months later they were married (Lorimer wrote, 'Picture yours truly supporting Willie Burrell as best man to the sweet strains of "the breath that breathed over Eden".') and went to Spain and Gibraltar for their honeymoon.

During these years William and his brother did not fail to keep an eye on the shipping world. In 1900–2 freight rates were very depressed, largely because of the release of so much tonnage from the transport services involved in the South African War. In 1902, after the signing of the peace treaty with the Boers, there was a short-lived boom before another depression occurred. In the same year William Burrell complained to Lorimer of the slump which he expected to bottom out in 1904. The two brothers were planning to re-activate the firm by repeating the formula which had already proved so successful. In 1905 they rocked the shipping world by placing contracts with Port Glasgow and Greenock yards for no fewer than twenty steamers in two batches of ten. These all joined the fleet of Burrell and Son in the course of 1906 and 1907, in company with the 'Fitzclarence III' and 'Fitzpatrick II', which came from Teeside yards. In order to superintend the building-up of the fleet and direct its operation William Burrell gave up his civic duties. Respect for the brothers' business acumen led other owners to follow suit and the resultant glut further depressed the market until matters reached a new low ebb in 1908 for shipbuilders (Lorimer's 'soup-kitchen times'). At this date ship plates were costing £6 7s 6d, thirty shillings less than the best price achieved in the previous year. Once again William and George were quick to take advantage of the situation and ordered another eight ships, which were delivered in 1909–10. The total of 34 vessels which comprised this new fleet was made up by a further four steamers built in 1912–13. As had been the case with the 1894 orders, the slump in the market enabled Burrell and Son to obtain the ships at rock-bottom prices; those delivered in 1906–7

SS 'Strathesk', built for Burrell and Son in 1909 by the Greenock and Grangemouth Dockyard Co. (Museum of Transport, Glasgow)

cost an average of £40,000 each. Changes in detail to the specifications took place between the ships ordered in the different years, but they all conformed to one basic design, incorporating all the latest developments in engineering and cargo handling. Each one was of approximately 4,400 gross tons with a length of about 375 feet, a breadth of 52 feet and a draught of 25 feet. They could carry up to 7,150 tons deadweight of goods in a cargo space of 380,000 cubic feet. Cargoes were handled by means of twelve derricks and ten steam winches and they were all equipped with electric lights. The boilers and triple-expansion engines were also an improvement on those installed in the 1894 fleet, giving a speed of about 12½ knots. The 'Strathesk II', built in 1909 by the Greenock and Grangemouth Dockyard Co., is a typical example of the new ships.

This fleet differed from the first one built up by William and George

Burrell, in that the old 64-share per ship system was abandoned in favour of limited liability. Each one of the new vessels was registered as a single company, e.g. 'The Strathesk Steamship Company Limited', with Burrell and Son appointed as managing directors. As such the firm received a management fee and also as shareholders benefited from the profits of the cargoes carried.

These profits must have been very considerable. Once again the cheap prices at which the ships had been built enabled Burrell and Son to undercut competitors; added to this advantage was the firm's excellent world-wide network of agents. The combination ensured that the ships operated with a minimum of ballast passages in a period of poor trading conditions in the shipping world in general.

In common with the earlier fleet, the new vessels with their British officers and Chinese and Lascar crews tramped the sea-routes of the globe. Coal was a cargo frequently carried world-wide and from the United States kerosene, grain and cotton were transported to Europe. Grain also came from Australia and cement was taken to the American Pacific ports and raw sugar from Fiji to Vancouver. Nitrates were transported from Chile to North America and Europe, and American lumber went to Europe, Australia and the Far East. There were few ports which did not see the house flag of Burrell and Son.

The commercial opportunism displayed by Burrell in former years was as much in evidence as ever. It is said that after the 1906 San Francisco earthquake the firm gained a monopoly on the carriage of building materials to the devastated city. This story has probably become exaggerated in the telling because it is difficult to believe that Burrell and Son could have been able to achieve this without much publicity, and none has been traced. The firm was involved in the relief work, for no fewer than four Burrell ships arrived at San Francisco during September and October of 1906 and cargoes were carried by the firm to this destination in the following year.

In 1912 trading conditions generally started to become healthier and there was a consequent rise in the market values of ships, a rise which became dramatic after the outbreak of the First World War. William and George decided to cash in on the situation and between 1913 and 1916 virtually the entire fleet was sold. The first sales took place before August 1914 and included two vessels which were still on the stocks. When hostilities commenced many of the fleet were chartered for war service and seven were lost through enemy action between 1914 and 1916. In the latter year most of the remaining ships were sold. Three were dispersed in single sales, six went to the Rome Steamship Company and ten were sold to the Commonwealth Government Line. The price for each of these ten was £145,000, which may be compared with the average construction cost of £40,000. The deal can be seen to have been even more favourable to Burrell and Son when one takes into account the fact that these steamers were between seven and ten years old and had already provided good returns on the original investment in the cargoes they had carried. Very few of these ships survived the War and most of those which did went to the breakers soon after or perished in the 1939–45 conflict. The two vessels which had been sold prior to completion in 1913 continued in service with different owners and under other names until 1959, thereby outlasting William Burrell.

At the end of the First World War Burrell and Son only owned two steamers, the 'Strathearn' and the 'Strathlorne'. The former was sold in 1919 but the 'Strathlorne' continued to trade until 1930. This ship was operated on a shoe-string. John Rioch, who served on it as junior engineer, recalled that it looked ready for the breakers' yard and there was seldom a voyage without a mechanical failure. John Rioch's elder brother Alex also worked for Burrell and Son in its last years as an office boy. One of his duties was to make out the accounts for provisions for the crew and he remembered how economically this was done. On being asked during 'The Millionaire Magpie' television programme whether he was surprised that Burrell was able to devote so much money to his art collecting, Alex Rioch replied that after his experience of the running of the ships it was 'no bloody wonder he had got that'.

It must be borne in mind that the experiences of the Rioch brothers date from a period when the firm's activities were running down. One suspects, however, that its vessels were always operated without frills or fancies. Some intimation of this is provided by a member of the family, who when talking about William Burrell's visit to Australia in the 1880's, drily observed:

> He *may* have booked his passage on one of Burrell and Son's ships, but somehow I think it more likely that he went by P. & O.

The firm stayed in business as agents and brokers on a reduced scale for another two decades after the sale of the 'Strathearn'. In 1927 George Burrell died and soon after that the offices in George Square were given up. For the last ten years of its existence it operated from 124 St Vincent Street, finally closing down in 1939. Although William Burrell continued to keep an eye on the firm's affairs to the end, he had to all intents and purposes retired when the bulk of the fleet was sold. With his share of the proceeds shrewdly invested he devoted the remainder of his long life to what became an all-consuming passion, the amassing of a vast art collection.

2

THE GLASGOW SCENE

It was an age of collectors who began young, who relied on their own study and judgement, and who contained in themselves a formidable body of knowledge.

Henry Hake

Archibald McLellan (1797–1854)
(Mitchell Library, Glasgow)

STRANGE as the notion may appear now, it is doubtful if during the 1890's there was anywhere in the United Kingdom outside London better equipped than Glasgow to provide anyone so inclined with an artistic education. Nor in this respect was it a disadvantage to have been born into a world of commerce. Glasgow at this time was at the height of its prosperity and expansion, earning the epithet of the 'Second City'. Some of those who controlled its commercial and industrial life utilised their fortunes in amassing art collections. During the late nineteenth century there were a number of collectors to be found in the ranks of the rich Scottish industrialists and ship-owners, building on the foundations laid by the Glasgow coachbuilder Archibald McLellan (1797–1854), that enlightened connoisseur and patron, whose paintings formed the nucleus of the fine collections at Kelvingrove Art Gallery. These collectors, many of whom were of Burrell's generation or only a few years older, numbered amongst them a wide range of interests. R.W. MacKenzie (b. 1857) was a partner in a bleaching firm near Perth. He not only collected ancient furniture and tapestries but he was interested in the techniques and one summer ran a tapestry school. It was MacKenzie who provided Robert Lorimer with his first major commission, the restoration of Earlshall. There was also T.G. Arthur (b. *c.*1857, d. 1907), whose father founded the well-known warehouse firm of Messrs Arthur and Co. of Queen Street, Glasgow. Arthur was a man with a keen interest in hunting, but who also amassed a fine collection of pictures, including works by Courbet, Degas, Matthew Maris and Whistler. Burrell described him as possessing 'a good flair for pictures'. Arthur shared his artistic tastes with another partner in the firm, Arthur Kay (b. early 1860's, d. 1939). In spite of his commercial career Kay stands a little apart from his contemporaries. For a start he had enjoyed a superior formal education, having been a student at Glasgow University and studied art during vacations in Paris, Hanover, Leipzig and Berlin. Kay was as strongly opinionated in municipal politics as in artistic matters. His anecdotes of collecting, *Treasure Trove in Art*, published posthumously, serve as a warning to all wealthy connoisseurs to avoid relating their experiences; although there is no record that Burrell ever commented on this book, it can be assumed with confidence that he disliked its braggardly and self-satisfied tone; it may even have reinforced his determination not to commit his memoirs to paper. Judging from his portrait by the Scottish painter James Elder Christie, Kay was somewhat of a dandy in appearance with a finely waxed and pointed moustache. In certain of his attitudes to art and collecting, he more closely resembles Burrell than any of the others. Like Burrell he claimed to have started whilst in his teens (with a seventeenth-century Dutch Old Master purchased at auction for his father) and he adopted a similar stance *vis-à-vis* academics and critics:

T.G. Arthur, drawn at the opening dinner of the 1883 exhibition of the Institute of Fine Arts. (Mitchell Library, Glasgow)

> A life of which the leisure, even in early youth, has been largely given to art, convinces me that the opinion of a dealer or collector, both of whom have paid for their own mistakes, is more valuable than that of people who spend their lives in criticising works of art in the purchase of, and payment for, which they have had neither risk, share, nor real responsibility. The way we gain good useful knowledge is by paying for our mistakes.

Burrell was to express exactly the same sentiments, albeit more succinctly. Kay was also as anxious as was Burrell to avoid alerting potential rivals to his interest in a particular work of art. Finally he was closest to Burrell in the scope of his collecting. Kay was an extremely discerning and wide-ranging connoisseur. He was particularly fond of the Old Masters, his early knowledge of whom was based on McLellan's paintings, and his collection included works by Rembrandt, Van Dyck, Saenredam and other Dutch seventeenth-century artists. In addition he owned over a hundred drawings by Tiepolo, a Goya and works by the leading eighteenth-century British artists, including Raeburn and Reynolds. His interests also extended to more recent times. He was an admirer of Matthew Maris, a leading member of the Hague School, and of the Barbizon painters. Although in general he avoided the more recent French painters, Kay together with T.G. Arthur were the first Scottish collectors to acquire works by Manet and Degas: in 1892 Arthur purchased Degas' *Chez la Modiste* (now in the Metropolitan Museum, New York) and Kay a *Repetition* and *L'Absinthe*, by the same artist. The last painting caused a storm of abuse when

A fellow-collector from early days: Arthur Kay (d. 1939). From an illustration in the Bailie, 20 March 1901. (Mitchell Library, Glasgow)

shown in London the following year on account of its 'low-life' subject-matter: it portrays a woman sitting in a café drinking absinthe. The controversy seems to have frightened both collectors, for very soon afterwards they sold their Degas pictures. Burrell was not aware of, or had forgotten, their early interest in this artist, for many years later he claimed that he was perhaps the first buyer of his works in Scotland.

Kay's collecting was not confined to paintings. He had more than two thousand pieces of English table glass and also liked bronzes, both of the Italian and German Renaissance and from China: his collection included examples from the Zhou, Han, Tang and Song dynasties.

Kay does not mention Burrell in his memoirs, neither did Burrell ever speak of him in his surviving correspondence, but their offices were very near and in the close-knit business world of Glasgow they must have known each other. They can hardly have been unaware of mutual artistic interests.

Although Kay was with the exception of Burrell perhaps the most catholic in his tastes of this generation of Scottish collectors, there were others who should be mentioned. Sir Thomas Gibson Carmichael (b. 1859), whose wealth was derived from Hailes quarry, near Edinburgh, possessed some fine Italian fifteenth and early sixteenth-century paintings and a splendid collection of medieval and Renaissance works of art, including Gothic ivories, enamels, English alabasters and tapestries. Some had been acquired from the well-known Magniac, Stein and Spitzer collections and several items were destined to find permanent homes in the British Museum and the Victoria and Albert Museum as well as the Burrell Collection. There were also a few magnificent and not so magnificent fakes.

Burrell knew Carmichael well and liked him very much. He also knew William Allen Coats (1853–1926), a partner in the thread manufacturing firm of J. & P. Coats of Paisley. An ardent devotee of yachting, he was no less passionate in his pursuit of art. Coats' enthusiasms in painting covered much the same ground as Arthur Kay. He owned some important Dutch Old Masters, including Vermeer's *Christ in the House of Martha and Mary*, which was later given to the National Galleries of Scotland by his two sons, and also liked the Hague and Barbizon Schools. His collection included no fewer than thirty works by Bosboom, twenty by Corot and four by Boudin. Coats also developed a strong liking for two painters who did not find favour with Kay: the highly individual Monticelli (1824–86) and the very different Joseph Crawhall (1861–1913). Included in the sale after his death were more than thirty works by the former and 46 by the latter.

These collections and that bequeathed by James Donald to Kelvingrove Art Gallery in 1905, are some of the most important of those formed by the wealthy Scottish merchants and industrialists in the late

Joseph Crawhall (Mitchell Library, Glasgow)

nineteenth and early twentieth centuries. To obtain a full appreciation of the very wide range and scope of their activities one has to look no further than the catalogue of the Glasgow International Exhibition of 1901; their outlook was far from parochial and narrow and a number of them, like Burrell, had ventured into the art world at a comparatively young age: T.G. Arthur had ceased collecting by the late 1890's and Coats' collection was largely formed in the same decade. Arthur Kay, as we have seen, also started young. In his introduction to Kay's *Treasure Trove in Art*, Henry Hake, Director of the National Portrait Gallery, wrote:

> It was an age of collectors who began young, who relied on their own study and judgement, and who contained in themselves a formidable body of knowledge.

Although there is considerable truth in this statement, it fails to acknowledge the rôle played by a group of discerning art dealers in interesting and educating their clients in new artists and fields. To adapt the comment applied to the famous dealer Duveen, they noticed that Europe had plenty of art and Glasgow had plenty of money.

Four of these dealers were particularly important. The Glasgow-born Daniel Cottier (1838–91) was by training a glass-painter. During his career as such he was responsible for some outstanding work and he collaborated with Alexander 'Greek' Thomson on the decoration of two of the latter's masterpieces, Queen's Park Church (destroyed in the Second World War by bombing) and Great Western Terrace. In 1869 Cottier moved to London and in partnership with several others founded the firm of Cottier & Co., 'Art Furniture Makers, Glass and Tile Painters'. The business went well and in 1873 branches in Australia and the United States were opened.

By this time Cottier had turned at least part of his attention to art dealing. As a young man in London he had attended lectures on fine art by Ruskin, Rossetti and Ford Madox Brown and developed a passion for painting, particularly the Barbizon School. As the Scottish critic W.G. Henley wrote:

> . . . he perceived, at a time when most critics were still cavilling or discussing, that the Nineteenth Century would be known, so far as art is concerned, as the century of that great school of painting whose finest and completest expression is the landscape of Corot.

Cottier was buying works by Corot, Courbet, Daubigny, Bonvin and others at a time when most other *savants* did not even suspect their existence and although no longer living in Glasgow he found a ready reception for them amongst Scottish collectors, and no less among the artists who were to form the group known as the 'Glasgow Boys'. In 1886 he introduced the collectors to Monticelli by showing eight of his paintings at the Edinburgh International Exhibition. Cottier had a particular liking for this artist and no fewer than 25 works by him were included in the posthumous sale of his collection. There were also twelve Corots, eleven Daubignys, and five Bonvins as well as paintings by other French artists. The Hague School was represented through several pictures by Bosboom and James Maris, but only two minor works of the latter's brother Matthew. This is at first rather surprising, for Matthew had lodgings in Cottier's house in St James's Terrace, Regents Park, for fifteen years from 1872, during which period he produced some of his finest paintings. Judging from his letters, however, the Dutch artist was very unhappy and complained that Cottier had kept him occupied on designing gas-globes and restoring Old Masters. By 1887 the antipathy between the two men had reached such a level that Maris left and was taken in hand by another dealer, his fellow-countryman Elbert van Wisselingh. He provided Maris with accommodation and a salary, leaving him free to paint whatever he liked. Van Wisselingh is a figure of some importance. His father had a small art gallery in Amsterdam, specialising in the Hague School painters. He placed his son at the Paris branch of Messrs Goupil, the international art dealers, where another employee was Vincent van Gogh. It was during his employment at Goupil that Elbert came to the notice of Cottier, who persuaded him to run his shop in London, concentrating on the Barbizon group. On his father's death in 1884 Elbert left Cottier's employ and took over and expanded the Amsterdam business. Nine years later he opened a branch in London, where he exhibited not only the works of the Hague School but also those of the Barbizon painters and contemporary British artists.

Although Van Wisselingh, who died in 1912, never had premises in Glasgow he had close personal ties with the 'Second City' in that he was married to a daughter of the dealer Craibe Angus (1830–99), who had opened his shop at 159 Queen Street in 1874. Angus was a very influential dealer in Scotland and shared Van Wisselingh's admiration for Matthew Maris. Their professional and personal association was a major factor in bringing his and the other Hague School artists' work to the attention of Scottish collectors. Angus also stocked the Barbizon painters. He seems to have had a business arrangement with Cottier by which they acted as each other's agents in Glasgow and London respectively.

The fourth of these dealers was Alexander Reid (1854–1928), who stood apart from the Cottier–Van Wisselingh–Angus axis, and was of greater significance in that he exerted a strong influence on the development of Burrell's artistic tastes. Many years later Burrell paid glowing tribute to him in a letter to his son, A.J. McNeill Reid:

> He did more than any other man has ever done to introduce fine pictures to Scotland and to create a love of art. He had a marvell-

Sir James Guthrie
(Mitchell Library, Glasgow)

ous flair for French 19th Century and when an exceptionally fine picture came along, he grew very excited. He went to a fine picture like a needle to a magnet and not even in Paris was there a better judge, and few of his equal. He was looked up to by the Paris dealers with the greatest respect.

Alexander Reid's father had founded a firm of carvers and gilders in Glasgow and in 1877 his son persuaded him to show pictures. Over the next few years he seems to have exhibited works by his friends amongst the rising group of Glasgow artists, including Guthrie, Walton and Crawhall, supplemented by a few foreign painters such as Corot and William Maris. His early tastes, in other words, reflected the current liking for the Hague and Barbizon Schools.

In 1887 his father decided that he should broaden his horizons and sent him to Paris to join the firm of Boussod and Valadon, which had bought out Goupil. Alex only remained a few months with Boussod and Valadon, but in that time he met and formed a close friendship with Theo van Gogh and his brother Vincent. The former ran a smaller gallery for the same firm and there Reid had the opportunity to see at first-hand works by Degas, Manet, Sisley, Pissarro, Toulouse-Lautrec and Gauguin, artists totally unknown in Glasgow at that time. For a while Reid shared an apartment with Vincent, in which period the latter painted two portraits of his friend which are the only ones in his *oeuvre* of a British sitter. So closely did the two men resemble each other that the two paintings were long assumed to be self-portraits of Vincent. The Scottish painter A.S. Hartrick (1864–1950) who knew them both at this time explained how close the resemblance was:

> The likeness was so marked that they might have been twins. I have often hesitated, until I got close, as to which of them I was meeting. They even dressed somewhat similarly, though I doubt if Vincent ever possessed anything like the Harris tweeds Reid usually wore.

Half a century later, when Van Gogh's paintings had for a long time commanded high prices, Burrell said that Reid had told him that at this time he could have bought anything the artist did for ten francs. This was a chance missed, for Reid did not handle any of Van Gogh's works until 1920. In any case the opportunity to buy so cheaply must have been of short duration because it was not long before Reid fell out with both Vincent and Theo. The cause of the quarrel was the interest shown by Reid and the Van Gogh brothers in Monticelli. The former it seems was determined to challenge Cottier's hold on the supply of this artist's works and the latter, who admired his colour and use of paint, were equally keen to corner the market. Vincent also hoped that Reid would try and sell Impressionist paintings in London and Glasgow, but the latter felt that he lacked the capital to purchase outright and

E.A. Walton by Harrington Mann (Mitchell Library, Glasgow)

Alexander Reid by Vincent van Gogh (Glasgow Museums and Art Galleries). Reid played a vital rôle in the formulation of Burrell's tastes in painting.

hesitated. The Van Goghs considered that Reid was too inclined to play safe, knowing that his profits on his Monticellis were assured. Vincent with his notoriously quick temper heatedly accused Reid of 'loving dead pictures and completely neglecting living artists'. Soon after his return to Glasgow, in March 1889 Reid opened his own gallery with the title of 'La Société des Beaux-Arts' at 232 West George Street, where he remained for five years; in 1894 the gallery moved to larger premises at 124 St Vincent Street and ten years later Reid returned to West George Street, at No 117. Once established, Reid, in Professor Pickvance's words, 'brought to art dealing a passionate commitment which meant that the affluent mercantile classes of Glasgow couldn't afford to ignore works of art.'

Almost from the outset he challenged the accepted tastes of Glaswegian collectors by introducing them to painters with which they were wholly unfamiliar. In February 1892 'La Société des Beaux-Arts' exhibited works by Degas, Monet, Pissarro and Sisley in addition to the better-known Monticelli and Courbet. The show was moderately successful and Alex Reid sold the three Degas pictures referred to earlier to Arthur and Kay. He also established a toe-hold for the Impressionists in Scotland: by 1895 at least three Monets, two Pissarros and two Sisleys were in Glasgow collections. Reid continued to support the Impressionists although fluctuations in the market and the conservatism of some of the collectors meant that he could not ignore the safer Barbizon and Hague Schools.

Reid did not concentrate solely on French and Dutch artists. In 1892 he met Whistler and although Craibe Angus had stocked some of his lithographs, Reid was the first Glasgow dealer to exhibit his paintings. Whistler was already known to the young artists forming the Glasgow Boys and exerted a strong influence on them. Reid continued his support of these painters, which he had already favoured before his sojourn in Paris. He negotiated exhibitions for the Glasgow Boys in Munich in 1890 and in the United States five years later. He also held several one-man shows in Glasgow, including two for Joseph Crawhall, in 1894 (the artist's first) and 1903. All in all, Reid's influence on the rather circumscribed art world of Glasgow in the 1890's and early part of the twentieth century was decisive in broadening its horizons. His impact in the years after the First World War was to be no less important, not least on Burrell.

3
EARLY COLLECTING

He . . . really has very fine taste (God knows where he got it and his knowledge from).

Robert Lorimer

IT is against the background outlined in the last chapter that Burrell's early collecting should be seen. He did not lack opportunity to study works of art at first-hand. In the homes of his business friends and acquaintances like W.A. Coats, Kay and Arthur were a wide range of paintings, including Old Masters and works by the Hague and Barbizon Schools; Kay also had Chinese bronzes, and superb medieval *objets d'art,* furniture and tapestries were owned by Sir Thomas Gibson Carmichael and R.W. MacKenzie. The market, at least in paintings, was serviced by dealers of discernment with good sources of supply. In the premises of Angus and Reid, situated within easy walking distance of the offices of Burrell and Son in George Square, fine pictures were readily available.

The first firm evidence of Burrell's collecting interests occurs in the last decade of the nineteenth century, when he was in his thirties, although even then our information is scrappy and incomplete. He apparently retained his youthful interest in portraiture, judging from notes on the files on two Dutch child pictures dated 1622 and 1635, which are still in the Collection; they were, according to these notes, purchased in Holland around 1890. This is interesting in revealing that Burrell, before he had even attained the age of thirty, was confident enough to chance his arm with Continental dealers. Unfortunately the evidence is of questionable value, in that no source is quoted on the files, although our knowledge of his collecting methods a few years later provides some measure of corroboration.

By the early 1890's, if not before, Burrell had developed a taste for the

Glasgow Boys, that loose-knit group of artists who turned their backs on the sentimental, romantic paintings produced by the previous generation (whom they derisively termed 'Gluepots') which were much in favour with the Royal Academy in London and Royal Scottish Academy in Edinburgh; the latter august body also incurred the wrath of the Boys for ignoring all painters who resided outside that city. Although the group included artists of widely differing aims, they had a common interest in realistic painting, and particularly in rendering the quality and effects of light. They were strongly influenced by the Barbizon and Hague Schools, with which some of the Glasgow Boys

4 THE AVIARY, CLIFTON by
Joseph Crawhall. Burrell was a
life-long admirer of this artist's
work and probably purchased this
water-colour after the one-man show
organised by Alex Reid in 1894.

6 The mother-of-pearl box 'with top
carved into fishes', described by
Robert Lorimer in one of his letters to
R.S. Dods.

5 'Poems in paint, full of feeling
and tenderness', was Burrell's
description of Matthew Maris's
pictures. This one, BUTTERFLIES,
was an early buy.

7 CHARITY OVERCOMING ENVY,
*the late 15th-century tapestry which
Burrell used to decorate the landing
of his home in Great Western
Terrace.*

8 *Another of the embellishments of
Great Western Terrace, Thomas
Couture's* LE CONVENTIONNEL.

9 *Burrell's first Degas:*
LA LORGNEUSE. *Bought from
Alex Reid in about 1901, Burrell
tried unsuccessfully to sell it soon
afterwards.*

11 STILL LIFE by François Bonvin, a
self-taught artist who specialised in
the portrayal of everyday life.

10 The finest of the examples in the
Collection of 18th-century British
portraiture, Hogarth's MRS ANNE
LLOYD.

12 STILL LIFE by Jean-Baptiste-
Simeon Chardin, one of the greatest
18th-century French painters.

Mary Burrell photographed beside her portrait with the artist, John Lavery. (Alan Mitchell)

'Gather ye rosebuds while ye may': a stained-glass panel by George Walton in Burrell's house at 4 Devonshire Gardens, which was commissioned by him in 1892. (Library of the Royal Institute of British Architects)

had come into contact through study in Paris, whilst others became acquainted with them through Cottier and Craibe Angus.

Burrell's first known acquisition of a work by a contemporary Scottish artist was not an easel painting, nor was it by a Glasgow Boy. It was a stained-glass panel commissioned early in 1892 for the large window lighting the stairs in his new house at 4 Devonshire Gardens, where much of it still remains intact. There is a relationship with the Glasgow Boys in that the artist, George Walton, was the brother of E.A. Walton, one of the leading lights of the School, but the design of this window owes nothing to the work of the Glasgow Boys, and very little to any contemporary stained glass artists. The theme is the familiar 'Gather ye rosebuds while ye may', with three young girls standing in a strange landscape with very formalised trees and plant forms. The colour of the

George Henry and E.A. Hornel by John Lavery (Mitchell Library, Glasgow)

glass is well-balanced and altogether the window is a highly successful composition. It shows that in this period, when he was still formulating his tastes, Burrell was adventurous and independent-minded enough to entrust a major commission to a largely unknown artist who was to play an influential role in the emergence of the distinctive 'Glasgow Style' in stained glass. This window is also significant in that it is the first indication of what was to be Burrell's life-long passion for the medium of stained glass.

Two years after he had ordered the Devonshire Gardens' window we find Burrell closely involved with the Glasgow Boys. This interest appears to have been carefully cultivated by Alex Reid, for in that year (1894) he invited Burrell to a supper party to celebrate his move to the St Vincent Street premises. All the leading members of the School were there, including Guthrie, Henry, Hornel, Kennedy, Lavery, Stevenson and E.A. Walton. Burrell retained happy memories of this occasion, for years later he proudly claimed that he was the only non-artist invited. Whether this was a reward for support already given or was intended to elicit future patronage is unclear, but it was in the same year that he commissioned Lavery to paint a full-length study of his favourite sister Mary. This was probably done to celebrate her twenty-first birthday which fell in 1894, although the portrait was not finished until the following year. Lavery was at the time a friend of the Burrell family and a photograph exists of the artist posing by the finished portrait with the sitter. Burrell also knew the handsome, outgoing Arthur Melville (1854–1904), although his first recorded purchase of one of his water-colours is as late as 1917 (there are five in the Collection today). Melville was particularly friendly with Joseph Crawhall and the Northumbrian-born artist's one-man show organised by Reid in 1894 made an immediate impact on Burrell. In his colourful autobiography *The Life of a Painter* Lavery recalled that W.A. Coats and Burrell were the chief buyers at this exhibition. It seems, however, that only one of the Crawhalls bought on this occasion, *The Aviary, Clifton*, is still in the Burrell Collection. Burrell always retained an admiration for this artist's skilled drawing style and there are many more works by him in the Collection than by any other painter. Alex Reid even complained that he had too many and what is more, that he would never part with them. Appropriately for one whose favourite subjects included hunting-scenes, in appearance Crawhall resembled a whipper-in. This was Lavery's description, who also said that he was of a silent disposition, hence his nickname 'The Great Silence', or less kindly, 'Creeps'. He could be witty on occasions, but the night when Burrell entertained him to dinner at home was not one of them: the artist ate a hearty meal then fell asleep until very late, when he had to be sent off in a cab.

At the same time as, under Reid's prompting, Burrell was taking an

See plate 4

interest in the Glasgow Boys, the same dealer was pointing him towards one of their mentors and the most advanced British painter of the period, James McNeill Whistler. Around the middle of the decade Burrell acquired two of Whistler's finest full-length pictures, *La*

Princesse du Pays de la Porcelaine, dated 1864, and the *Fur Jacket,* the latter being a portrait of the artist's current model and mistress Maud Franklin. The former was purchased by Reid at Christie's in 1892 and he was urged by the painter himself to sell it abroad:

> . . . I hope in any case you will send her to Chicago. There is where all the thousands will come to you for these pictures of mine, and I *do* want them to go out of England. Do ask £2000 – *and don't sell it to an Englishman.*

In the event it was purchased by a Scotsman in the person of William Burrell, although the picture was eventually to end up in an American gallery.

There are two versions of the circumstances surrounding Burrell's acquisition of the *Fur Jacket.* The more recent appeared in the Glasgow Herald for 29 July 1959. According to this the picture was owned by a syndicate led by Reid and which included Craibe Angus. It was Angus who persuaded Burrell to buy it for £400 and he took £60 commission. The second account, by Neil Munro in *The Brave Days,* has it that Whistler sold the picture to Reid for £400 on the understanding that if and when the latter disposed of it half the profits should go to the painter. Some years later Reid sold it to Burrell for £1,000 and Whistler claimed his half-share of £300. It has not proved possible to verify either story.

Although Reid managed to interest Burrell in the Glasgow Boys and such an *avant-garde* artist as Whistler he signally failed to persuade him to buy any of the Impressionist paintings by Monet, Pissarro and Sisley which he had shown in Glasgow in 1892. Nor was he successful at this time in getting him to appreciate the merits of Degas. Possibly he was put off by the notoriety *L'Absinthe* attracted and with the exception of one picture acquired around 1901 he was only to start buying works by this artist towards the end of the First World War. Indeed it cannot be said that even with Reid's prompting Burrell was amongst the most adventurous of the Scottish collectors in the 1890's; in some areas he already knew what he didn't like, and this included *plein-air* Impressionism. With a few isolated (but important) exceptions the Impressionist painters were never to appeal to him in a lifetime of collecting.

See plate 24

Burrell did acquire works by other French painters from Reid in the 1890's. These included a Monticelli, *The Bazaar, Marseilles,* Manet's *Portrait of Victorine Meurent* and Daumier's *The Artist at his Easel.* In 1899 he purchased Daumier's *Suzanne et les Vieillards* and two Whistlers, *Nocturne* and *Paysage;* the price of the first was £120, and the last two were £85 each. He had not lost his interest in eighteenth-century British portraiture, for in the same year Reid sold him a study by Raeburn of the head of an old lady.

Burrell almost certainly had other paintings from Reid in this period, but our knowledge is incomplete as none of the latter's stockbooks prior to 1899 has survived. Reid was not the only dealer from whom the young ship-owner bought. From notes in the Burrell Collection records it appears that he also bought from Craibe Angus and Van Wisselingh. It would be surprising if Burrell ignored them as it will be recalled that the former's gallery was close to the offices of Burrell and Son. Leaving aside the dubious case of the *Fur Jacket*, Burrell apparently acquired four lithographs by Whistler from Angus; he also obtained through Van Wisselingh one of the painter Johan Barthold Jongkind's finest pictures, *Fabrique de Cuirs Forts*. Angus and Van Wisselingh mainly sold Burrell works by the brothers James and Matthew Maris. Burrell at this time favoured the Hague School as much if not more than any other group of painters. Three pictures by James Maris and no fewer than twelve by Matthew Maris are noted in the Burrell Collection files as having been acquired from this source. Burrell always remained an admirer of Matthew Maris. In 1945, a strongly-worded reply to an implied criticism of this taste by Tom Honeyman, the Director of Glasgow Museums and Art Galleries, contains a passage in which Burrell, for once, waxed lyrical:

> He [Matthew Maris] is not everybodys painter but, nevertheless, he was a great genius. He was a dreamer and his pictures are poems in paint, full of feeling and tenderness and it was because I liked his work so much I bought it.

See plate 5

Notwithstanding the sparse and patchy evidence considerable light can be shed on Burrell's interests in pictures before he was forty. To his early liking for seventeenth and eighteenth-century portraiture had been added an admiration for Monticelli, the Hague School and the Glasgow Boys, whose works were readily accessible in the galleries of Glasgow art dealers and the homes of wealthy mercantile collectors. In addition, under Reid's tuition, he had been attracted to Whistler and although he preferred low-toned pictures and therefore the Impressionists did not appeal to him, the purchase of the Manet reveals that he was beginning to venture into seas largely uncharted by other Scottish connoisseurs. Moreover Burrell's collecting was by no means confined to the medium of painting; at the same time he was active in an area far removed from that of eighteenth and nineteenth-century pictorial art, as is evidenced by Lorimer's correspondence with Dods. It is apparent from Lorimer's first letter about Burrell, which was quoted in Chapter 1, that the latter had already by early 1898 been collecting in the fields of Late Gothic and Renaissance decorative and applied arts of Northern Europe. It reveals too not only that Burrell owned seventeen paintings by Matthew Maris, which is more than is known from the Angus–Van Wisselingh notes, but also that he was already smitten with the idea of baronial living and was collecting furniture and objects of the appropriate period (the brass dishes referred to by Lorimer are examples of a type of ware made in large numbers in Nuremberg in the early sixteenth century). Moreover, if with paintings he was to some extent guided by Reid and perhaps Angus, with the decorative arts he was willing to cast his net wider. Towards the end of his life Burrell recalled that in his early days as a collector 'I bought [in Paris] from Tempelaere, Bernhard, Feinard and other dealers whose names I have now forgotten.'

Details of only one of Burrell's *objets d'art* purchases before 1900 have come down to us. Many years later he told Muirhead Moffat, a well-known Glasgow antique dealer, that he had bought a very rare Chelsea porcelain figurine of Isabella d'Andreini in 1892 from a London dealer for £5. This disclosure was prompted by an offer of £4,000 for the piece from another collector. Burrell refused to sell and the figurine, one of his few gestures towards the Baroque, continues to grace the Collection.

Lorimer observed Burrell at first-hand over the next few years. In September 1898 he accompanied the Burrell family on a fortnight's trip to the Netherlands:

> The party consisted of Burrell . . . his mother, a fine old Trojan of 64, his two sisters and a friend of B's called Mitchell, an extremely nice young chap, 6 in all.

A photograph of the group was taken on this holiday, with Mrs Burrell wearing mourning, which gave her a close resemblance to Queen Victoria. This 'nice young chap' was James Alexander Ralston Mitchell, who was to marry Mary Burrell three years later. They travelled through the countryside visiting Flushing, Haarlem, Rotterdam and Amsterdam before returning via Antwerp. The mecca for Burrell was Amsterdam, with its rich antique shops. He did not fail to apply the

The Chelsea porcelain figurine of Isabella d'Andreini. Bought by Burrell for £5, he later refused an offer for it of £4,000.

The family party on the 1898 trip through Holland. Lorimer and Burrell are in the centre; Burrell's mother, looking extraordinarily like Queen Victoria, is on the far right.

commercial skills and business acumen learned in the hard world of shipping to his dealings with the Dutch art trade:

> It was very interesting going round all the shops with Burrell, and I think I can say that I know the ropes in the way of antique shops.

Lorimer made a few purchases at half what he had expected to pay.

> . . . this was all thanks to Burrell, the man's a perfect nailer. A.1 taste very humerous [sic] and ready witted, and any amount of chaff . . . To see him tackling some of [the] picture dealers was a treat. . . .

Burrell also found time to buy on his business travels. On at least one of these he was spurred by one of Lorimer's fancies:

> You never saw such a chap as that Burrell. He's been all over the place on business since we were in Holland, I put him onto pearl to show him its charms. Coming here I went out to see him in the evening – [he] went out and opened a cabinet saying I'll show you something, and here are more pearl boxes [which he had] collected in these weeks than I've got in 5 years!! and some lovely bits, a box with top carved into fishes – I did covet, but then he'd been through every shop in Paris Rouen and Havre God knows where else. I've been teaching him too much! *See plate 6*

In July 1899 a sale took place of the contents of a Dutch Castle:

> B. was in the place a year ago – says its crammed with fine stuff the accumulation of 300 years, wants me to go over to the sale with him. If I can get away and he pays the shot, of course I will. But 'not being a collector' – I won't go on my own hook, but he has fairly set me on fire with accounts of the gothic hanging candelabras he saw.

It is not known whether Burrell acquired anything at this sale, but soon after he and Lorimer spent another holiday in the Low Countries, where they visited Dordrecht, Gouda, Meppel, Utrecht, Delft and Brussels. Both men added to their collections on this trip.

Lorimer told his eldest son Christopher how Burrell used to set about his task on his travels:

> When we arrived at our hotel the first thing that Willie Burrell did was to ask the hotel porter to make up a list with the names and addresses of *every* antique shop in the town. When this was completed we ordered a cab and went round all the dealers.

By now Burrell, having divested himself of the fleet, could devote more and more time to his personal interests as well as his civic duties. In 1900 he went to Paris, evidently without Lorimer, where he viewed an international exhibition of important tapestries, sculpture and arms and armour. Burrell's pencilled notes in the catalogue indicate how closely he studied the exhibits. His copy of the catalogue also has a brief record of some purchases he made on this trip. They include an English fifteenth-century alabaster panel depicting the Adoration of the Magi, and a polychromed wooden figure of Christ from a Flagellation scene taken from a Flemish altarpiece, in addition to three Hispano–

Moresque plates and a fragment of a Gothic tapestry; the alabaster panel and the Christ figure are still in the Collection.

Early in September of the same year the Burrell family went abroad again, accompanied by Lorimer. He looked forward eagerly to this holiday, because as he confided to Dods, Burrell was '. . . a rare guide and dead keen on the fine things both in the shops and in the museums and galleries'.

One of the places they visited was the picturesque medieval town of Rothenburg-ob-der-Tauber, where Mary Burrell and James Alexander Ralston Mitchell became engaged. This happy family event is unlikely to have deflected Burrell from his study of the art treasures in the churches of the town and neighbourhood, particularly Tilman Riemenschneider's masterpiece, the Holy Blood retable, and the stained glass to be seen in St Jakob's church. Lorimer does not record whether Burrell purchased any Gothic works of art, but noted that he did buy a large quantity of Roman glass.

In June 1901 Burrell announced his engagement to Constance Mitchell and although Lorimer foresaw that the marriage would eventually put an end to their travels abroad, this did not happen immediately. Moreover, as we shall see presently Burrell's purchase of a marital home was to add a business relationship to their close friendship.

The year 1901 is also of major significance in reconstructing Burrell's early collecting. Even with the Lorimer–Dods correspondence there are considerable blanks in our knowledge, but now, for the first time and at the moment when Burrell was moving into middle age, an overall view of his interests can be obtained. The occasion was the

The Princess Royal, HRH Princess Louise, Duchess of Fife, at the opening of the 1901 Glasgow International Exhibition. Though Burrell was a member of the organising committee, he does not appear to be in this photograph – perhaps another example of his avoiding the limelight.
(Mitchell Library, Glasgow)

Glasgow International Exhibition held at Kelvingrove in that year. Burrell was a member of the General Committee and served on three of the sub-committees responsible for the art section. Although the Exhibition included works in the possession of such established collectors as Arthur, Kay, W.A. Coats and Sir Thomas Gibson Carmichael, Burrell was the largest single lender with more than two hundred works. Even taking into account the glimpses of his activities in the previous decades the range and scope of his acquisitions are astonishing and show that he was already a collector of major standing in Scotland.

In addition to certain fields in which he is known to have been active from earlier sources, such as Nuremberg dishes and Roman glass, there are others which come as a complete surprise. These include nearly fifty articles of sixteenth and eighteenth-century Dutch, German and Venetian table glass, a few items of silver, some antique furniture, nine Persian rugs and carpets, and two bronzes by Rodin and Van der Stappen.

Even in the better-documented areas discoveries emerge from the catalogue. In company with the two Whistler portraits and works by Crawhall (4) and James and Matthew Maris (10), etc. some names appear for the first time. These include several Old Masters, comprising two prints by Dürer and Cranach the Elder and a portrait of the Infanta Maria Theresa attributed optimistically to Velasquez; and the list of Hague School artists is augmented by the name of Bosboom. The greatest surprise is afforded by the ranks of French artists, where Manet, Monticelli, Daumier and Jongkind are joined by Thomas Couture, Géricault, Bargue and Ribot (it seems that at this time Burrell owned six works by Daumier, the largest single collection of his paintings in the British Isles). Another new name is Phil May (d. 1903), who

was represented by seven works. May is best known for his *Punch* cartoons, and his virtuoso skills as a draughtsman were admired by Lavery and Whistler. Burrell was probably attracted by that mastery of line which he had in common with Crawhall. It is doubtful if the conservative art collector would have approved of May's extremes of dress; Lavery related how the last time he met May, he was wearing a very loud suit. Not in the least abashed, May invited him 'to come in and listen to it, dear boy'.

Perhaps the most remarkable of Burrell's loans to the 1901 Exhibition are the medieval items. They may have lacked the individual quality of Sir Thomas Gibson Carmichael's objects, but they form an important and coherent group. The only Gothic items specifically identified in Burrell's possession before 1901 are the tapestry, the alabaster Adoration and the wooden Christ which he purchased in Paris the previous year. Both the sculptures appear in the Exhibition, accompanied by no fewer than thirteen tapestries, mainly of fifteenth and sixteenth-century date (Burrell's mother also loaned three), about the same number of carvings in ivory and wood and a large quantity of brass household and liturgical objects, including altar candlesticks, a cross and a chalice. Finally, Burrell loaned three large panels of stained glass and an unspecified number of Swiss sixteenth and seventeenth-century small panels. Some of these may have been obtained from Grosvenor Thomas (1856–1923), a Glasgow Boy who turned to dealing, principally in stained glass; after the First World War Burrell made some major acquisitions from him.

By any standards his loans cover an extraordinarily wide range of artistic activity both in date and culture. Yet Burrell did not exhibit everything in his collection. For example, none of the pictures by Whistler, Raeburn and Daumier which he acquired from Alex Reid in 1899 was shown. It is also important to note that most of the areas in which he was to collect for the rest of his long life were well-represented and they demonstrate that the shape of the Collection was already formed.

When the Exhibition opened Burrell was still living with his mother at 4 Devonshire Gardens, but soon after he acquired a new home for his bride and himself (his mother remained in his old house until her death in 1912). This was not as might be expected the baronial country residence after which he had been hankering for some time. As recently as 1899 he had made a determined attempt to buy just such a place, as Lorimer told Dods:

> Do you remember the old ruin hanging right over the sea near St Monans, called Newark Castle. Burrell has been wanting it for years but I've always dissuaded him, but when he was staying here [at Kellie] we went down to see it, and I came to see that it

Burrell's baronial dream: Lorimer's impression of Newark Castle in Fife as it might have appeared after restoration. Nothing came of it as the owner refused to sell. (Royal Commission on the Ancient and Historical Monuments of Scotland)

could be made a place of, so I roughly measured it up and made sketch plans – a nailing plan look at my great vista, with the end window of the Dining room looking right out to sea, and such views there are, and the way my gate house garden walls etc. is all to work out is immense.

The site on the Fife coast was splendid and Lorimer's sketch shows what a romantic building might have emerged, but the owner, a Mr Baird of Elie, could not be persuaded to sell. Lorimer still retained hopes of getting it for Burrell but it was not to be. When Burrell eventually found his castle it was one which could not compare with Newark and Lorimer's involvement was to prove fatal to their friendship.

In 1901 all this was in the distant future. The house Burrell purchased was in elegant Great Western Terrace, designed by 'Greek' Thomson and only a few yards from Devonshire Gardens. For someone who never seems to have been in sympathy with Neo-classicism it is a curious choice, even more so as he immediately called in Lorimer to re-model the interior in order to provide a suitably Gothic *ambience* for his oak furniture and medieval tapestries and *objets d'art*.

Burrell briefed Lorimer to make the interior as simple as possible and to 'chip away the gingerbread' as he put it. Lorimer carried out the work while Burrell was on honeymoon in Gibraltar. The walls were panelled in linenfold and Lorimer designed new Gothic-style fireplaces and a staircase in similar style. The stair newels had heraldic beasts and Lorimer also provided a double bed in Flemish Late Gothic fashion. A serious disagreement between the two men soon arose, however. Burrell's main concern was that the re-furbishing should enhance his objects and paintings and not reduce them to the level of interior decoration by arranging them as a harmonious scheme. Lorimer as an architect saw matters differently, as he explained to Dods:

> I've often told you what a fine collection of stuff he has, but he has no idea of the really far on way to arrange a house.

Lorimer was concerned that 'there should be no feeling of the curiosity shop', and no doubt pointed out to Burrell the desirability of subordinating what he felt were the details, i.e. Burrell's objects, to the overall effect.

The upshot was that Burrell was unhappy with Lorimer's alterations. The architect stayed there at the beginning of January 1902 and wrote that he had

> at last got him to enthuse a bit over his house . . . seeing his gothic tapestries hung up in his diningroom was what did it, his dining-room is now to be tapestry all round. The three gothic hunting scenes he had in the Glasgow exhibition just fill one side and he's going to have a tear round the continent in the spring to try and find some more.

The disagreements over Great Western Terrace were resolved amicably enough and Lorimer accompanied Burrell to Paris to find a tapestry to complete the dining room. Eventually they came across a Franco–Flemish one which was 'exactly the right size, 14′ 6″ long × 9ft high, of a seigneur in his park au promenade, with the lady on his arm, little children bathing in a pool and others riding on sheep and tilting at each other with toy windmills.'

The alterations proceeded slowly and Lorimer complained:

> The Burrell house is going to drive me into an early grave – its awful the amount of trouble and worry that has been expended on the work and it ain't done yet.

Progress must have been hindered by Burrell's obsessive attention to details on the one hand and, judging from Lorimer's comments on the dining room, his inability to make up his mind about the final arrangement of the contents. Burrell's concern for relatively minor matters is illustrated by the cradle he got Lorimer to design for the child his wife was expecting (this was to be their only child, Marion, born in August 1902 – she has recently changed her name to Silvia).

> Isn't he a record breaker? Think of going into the question of a cradle with such thoroughness, 2 or 3 months before the kid is due! Last Sunday was wet and drew the whole thing out full size. Have put a hound on top of the pillar at the foot, and the pelican in her piety on the one at the top. . . . brushed out with wire brushes and fumed. It's own mother won't know it from a piece of French Gothic, late 15th century as they always label this stuff at S K [the Victoria and Albert Museum].

The Burrells moved into 8 Great Western Terrace at the end of June. After a visit made some six weeks later Lorimer commented to Dods that Burrell had

> hardly hung up anything. Got it too bare, in fact, but its on the right side to err on. The diningroom looks very fine. The whole place hung with the finest gothic tapestries, and in the centre a gothic table by yours truly. Some good chairs and that's about all. He dines off the bare board, and I must say I am old fashioned enough not to like it. I think there is something sacramental about the 'cloth'.

A series of photographs taken of the interior around 1905–6 show Burrell's collection arranged in the various rooms. In the entrance hall was a painting by Cranach the Elder of *Cupid and Venus*. Three Gothic statuettes, one of which was the Christ he purchased in Paris in 1900, stood on a wooden mantelpiece. The sitting room contained an early sixteenth-century Brussels tapestry, Chippendale chairs, a Malines Virgin and Child sculpture and in the windows, a series of sixteenth and seventeenth-century Dutch and Swiss stained-glass panels. In the dining room were hung the tapestries which had been the subject of much deliberation between Burrell and Lorimer. These included the

Burrell's wife Constance and
their daughter Marion.
A T.&R. Annan photograph of
about 1905.

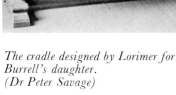

The cradle designed by Lorimer for
Burrell's daughter.
(Dr Peter Savage)

'Seigneur' tapestry purchased in Paris and several which were loaned
to the 1901 Exhibition. Altogether there were no fewer than seven
tapestries displayed in this room, which was not big enough to do them
justice. Tapestries of such large dimensions were designed for great
halls and with space between them; at Great Western Terrace they
were huddled together and appeared constricted. Other fittings
included two Gothic-style brass candelabra and some Swiss stained
glass. The furniture was sixteenth and seventeenth-century, in addition
to a set of Chippendale chairs. Decorating the staircase and landing

Part of the entrance hall at 8 Great Western Terrace showing Cranach's CUPID AND VENUS and, on the left above the fireplace, the wooden figure of Christ purchased in Paris in 1900. The photograph was taken around 1905–06.

The dining room at 8 Great Western Terrace around 1905–06.

were three more tapestries, including a fine late fifteenth-century French example representing *Charity overcoming Envy*, a Rodin bronze *(L'Amour qui passe)*, some Gothic sculpture and several paintings, of which the most important were Cranach the Elder's *Stag Hunt* and Couture's *Le Conventionnel*. Finally, set in the landing window were three early sixteenth-century German stained-glass panels depicting SS Peter, Paul and Nicholas.

See plate 7

See plate 8

Burrell's entire collection was not all on view in 8 Great Western Terrace and there are some important omissions from the 1905–6 photographs. Not least are the two Whistlers, *Fur Jacket* and *La Princesse du Pays de la Porcelaine*, and the Manet *Portrait of Victorine Meurent*, all of which he had acquired from Reid in the 1890's. The reason is that they had been sold. In May and June 1902 Burrell sent nearly forty pictures for auction at Christie's, including the Manet portrait, the Jongkind, four Daumiers, three Monticellis and several Hague School works.

See plate 9

Also his first Degas, *La Lorgneuse*, which he had only very recently obtained from Reid, and a study by Whistler for a head of Miss Cicely Alexander. The other two Whistlers were not in either of these sales, but they were disposed of soon afterwards.

Quite what impelled Burrell to sell his paintings at the moment he moved into Great Western Terrace is not certain. Possibly he felt that his primarily nineteenth-century collection was not suited to the 'Gothic' interior of his new home, or even that there was insufficient wall-space. A hint is contained in a letter which he wrote forty years later referring to one of the Monticellis that shortage of cash was a motive ('I had to sell'); possibly his new home was costing more than he expected, but it is more likely that he was trying to raise capital for the new fleet which he and his brother George were already planning to have built.

If Burrell hoped to realise a large sum he was doomed to disappointment, for many of the pictures put up for auction failed to realise their reserves and were bought in, including the Jongkind and the Degas. Unfortunately some of the best *were* sold and now grace various galleries in the United States, including Manet's *Victorine Meurent* which hangs in the Museum of Fine Arts, Boston. On some of the sales Burrell did make a considerable profit: *La Princesse du Pays de la Porcelaine*, for example, went to the American collector C.L. Freer in August 1903 for £3,750; Reid had obtained it for 420 guineas and it is unlikely that he made more than a modest profit from selling it to Burrell. Burrell would have been delighted to have washed his hands of one of the pictures which went overseas, had he known it was a forgery. This was *Don Quixote and the Windmills*, 'signed' by Daumier, which eventually passed into the ownership of the Art Institute, Chicago.

Whatever his motives were in trying to sell so many pictures, he had

An early escape: DON QUIXOTE AND THE WINDMILLS 'signed' by Daumier and since recognised as a fake. Burrell sold it in 1902. (Art Institute of Chicago)

no intention of ceasing to collect and it may be that the proceeds of the sales were earmarked for this purpose. In the early months of 1902, at the same time as the preparations for the sale of the paintings were in hand, Burrell purchased from Alex Reid a *Church Interior* by Van Vliet, in addition to the medieval tapestry bought in Paris. Only three days before the first of the sales he attended the sale of Sir Thomas Gibson Carmichael's collection and purchased the Cranach *Cupid and Venus*, which as we have seen he placed in the entrance hall at 8 Great Western Terrace, and two Italian paintings. He also acquired at the Gibson Carmichael sale the *Charity overcoming Envy* tapestry, which he hung on the landing at Great Western Terrace. Notwithstanding these excellent acquisitions, the impression remains that Burrell could have done much better at this sale. He was certainly aware of the possibilities it presented, for on 1 May he urged Glasgow Corporation to buy from the Carmichael Collection:

> I know the collection well and to my mind it is without exception the finest private collection in Scotland. I understand that . . . everything is to be sold without any reserve and I think that it is a *great* opportunity for the Council to acquire beautiful works at very moderate prices and prices which will be far below what they cost.

In the event Burrell himself missed the opportunity to obtain some very desirable medieval ivories and enamels, even leaving aside those items which were sufficiently important to be purchased by the British Museum and the Victoria and Albert Museum.

Little is known of Burrell's forays into the art world for almost a decade after the Gibson Carmichael sale. Although his commercial activities may have occupied most of his attention, the occasional gleam of light shows that his collecting did not cease. In 1903 Burrell persuaded his mother to sit for the former Glasgow Boy-turned fashionable portrait painter George Henry. The task gave the artist some trouble and his first attempt was so unsatisfactory that he scored it out and started anew. The Burrell family always considered that the first

Henry's portrait of Burrell's mother. It conveys very well her formidable personality.

See plate 10

version was the more successful of the two. The decidedly Whistlerian overtones of the final portrait perhaps served as an uncomfortable reminder to Burrell of the loss of his two masterpieces, the *Fur Jacket* and *La Princesse du Pays de la Porcelaine*.

His painting purchases at the Gibson Carmichael sale show that Burrell was not just interested in nineteenth-century and more recent schools, but that the works of earlier artists appealed to him. A few years later he bought one of several versions of the *Stag Hunt* painted by Cranach the Elder and Hogarth's fine portrait of *Mrs Ann Lloyd*; the latter was obtained from a Bond Street art gallery on Alex Reid's advice. The Dutch seventeenth-century school still exercised its attractions. In February 1905 he purchased from Reid a work by an unknown artist identified as Van Harlaem and five years later he made a successful bid at Christie's for a female portrait then attributed to Ludolph de Jongh and now considered to be the work of Jakob van Loo.

The few paintings and the one tapestry mentioned above represent all Burrell's known purchases in the period 1902–11, but they are unlikely to be the sum total. There are in the Collection a considerable number of pictures, including works by Bonvin, Boudin, Chardin, Corot, Crawhall, Daumier and others for which there is no record of acquisition and as they are not mentioned in the Purchase Books they may have been obtained before the middle of 1911. From then onwards for the first time we are on sure ground. Up to this point the only information available has been gleaned from a haphazard collection of sources, such as dealers' records, the 1901 Glasgow Exhibition and some of Burrell's letters written in his later years. If Burrell himself kept any formal record of his early acquisitions it has not survived or has not yet come to light. But in May 1911, shortly before his fiftieth birthday, that all changed. From the end of that month onwards, he kept detailed records of his expenditure in school exercise books. They number 28 and continue down to his last acquisitions in 1957, the year before he died. He made almost all the entries himself, except for the last few months when failing eyesight forced him to delegate the task to others. These Purchase Books are an invaluable record of the remarkable range and scale of his collecting.

Although the entries became more detailed as the years went by the basic format was established on the first page of the first book. There are separate columns for the date of acquisition, from whom the item was acquired, the price, date of delivery, insurance and whether photographed. The last column is headed 'All in Order' and usually has Burrell's initials by each entry.

Contrary to what one might have expected the early Purchase Books

See plates 11 and 12

The first page of the first Purchase Book. The annotations giving the Registration Numbers were made by Bill Wells, who became Keeper of the Collection in January 1956.

record only a few pictures and no medieval works of art; instead they are concerned almost exclusively with Chinese ceramics and bronzes, a field in which Burrell appears to have shown no interest before 1901, although in 1948 he told Andrew Hannah, then Keeper of the Collection, that he had been collecting bronzes 'from about the time I was 20', i.e. 1881. His memory, however, let him down occasionally in his last years and this statement may not be quite accurate. He certainly owned Chinese ceramics as early as *c*. 1905–6, for one of the photographs taken of 8 Great Western Terrace at this time shows three *famille noire* Kangxi wares on the drawing-room mantelpiece. We can only speculate as to what prompted this new and very different interest, which henceforward was to be of major importance. He may have seen the splendid collection of blue and white porcelain placed on loan in 1891 at the Victoria and Albert Museum by George Salting (1839–1909); equally he may have known through business contacts the collections of William Hesketh Lever, later Lord Leverhulme (d. 1924) and of George Eumorfopolous (1863–1939), although none of these contained bronzes. It is more likely that Burrell became familiar with Oriental art through studying examples in two collections on his doorstep. Leonard Gow (1859–1936), head of the shipping firm of Gow, Harrison & Co., possessed an important collection of Chinese porcelain, mainly of the Kangxi period, some of which Burrell was later to acquire. But his early purchases correspond most closely with Arthur Kay's interests. Both men had a liking for Chinese bronzes and Burrell in the first five years of the Purchase Books acquired more bronzes than he did ceramics. He always preferred bronzes, as a letter written in 1947 shows:

> . . . Chinese bronzes have always appealed to me to be far ahead of Pottery–Stoneware or Porcelain with perhaps the exception of the Prehistoric pieces.

The Chinese ceramics that were added to the Collection between 1911 and 1916 were quite diverse, with the Zhou, Han, Tang, Ming and Kuing dynasties each represented by a few pieces. The vendors were a group of specialist dealers in London, such as T.J. Larkin and Bluett and Son, although he also bought from a Paris dealer in January 1912. The Purchase Books contain sketches by Burrell of a number of the pieces, but they are too rough and ready and the written descriptions too brief, for many of the Chinese acquisitions to be identified with objects still in the Collection. A small group of paintings bought at the Cress Sale at Christie's in July 1915 are easily recognisable. It includes

See plate 13

the fifteenth-century School of Lorraine *Ecce Homo* and the *Annunciation* by the Master of the Brunswick Diptych which are amongst the treasures of the early pictures in the Collection.

The level of expenditure recorded in the Purchase Books for these early years is low and the acquisitions are somewhat sporadic. From

1911 to 1914 Burrell spent an average of £500 per annum, with the lowest amount occurring in 1914. For this year there is only one entry, on 9 February, when eight items were purchased for £42. In 1915 the graph of Burrell's spending starts to rise, but it was only from the beginning of February in the following year that a really dramatic change takes place in the scale and nature of the entries in the Purchase Books, coinciding with the sale of the bulk of Burrell and Son's fleet. The amounts spent are:

1915 : £1,172	1917 : £15,422
1916 : £3,257	1918 : £13,163

From February 1916 the somewhat casual acquisitions of Chinese ceramics and bronzes are overwhelmed by a flood of purchases from a wide variety of sources, comprising furniture, fittings, embroideries and paintings. The common thread running through them was the fact that they all demanded a large setting. Burrell already had sufficient furniture to fill 8 Great Western Terrace; now he had another project in mind, nothing less than a revival of his earlier scheme to live in a baronial residence. Off and on the achievement of this ambition was to occupy his attention for the next decade and cost him dearly, not just in financial terms but in his closest friendship.

The 15th-century painting ECCE HOMO, bought by Burrell at Christie's in 1915.

4

HUTTON CASTLE

I must leave you to enjoy the very untidyest arrangement you are insistent on . . .

Robert Lorimer

AS Burrell divested himself of his shipping interests after the outbreak of the First World War he no longer found it necessary to live in Glasgow. At the same time his greatly expanded collecting activities were far outstripping the space available at 8 Great Western Terrace and it became imperative to find a larger house. With his interest in tapestries and medieval sculpture it is not surprising that his old desire for baronial-style living was re-kindled. Another factor which must have appealed to Burrell's shrewd business brain was the depressed state of the property market; as ever he was after a bargain. What he ended up with was nothing like as romantic or as grand as Newark Castle, which he had been so keen to acquire before the turn of the century. In September 1915 Lord Tweedmouth placed on the market his estate at Hutton Castle in Berwickshire, eight miles from Berwick-on-Tweed, and Burrell acquired it soon after. At the time it must have seemed ideal. The estate comprised nearly 2,000 acres of good agricultural land which enabled him to offer shooting and fishing facilities matching those of his gentlemanly neighbours. A further attraction may have been its proximity to the area around Howtel in Northumberland where the Burrells had established themselves centuries earlier.

The castle is spectacularly situated in a commanding position overlooking the river Whitadder and had the colourful history typical of so many Border fortresses. In 1296 Edward I's army encamped at Hutton and exactly two hundred years later it was devastated by the Earl of Surrey during his punitive raid on Scotland in retaliation for James V's

—92—

support of the pretender Perkin Warbeck. At this time Hutton had long been owned by the Home family and it was still in its possession in 1544 when further disaster overtook it at the hands of the English. On 24 September Lord Eure, governor of Berwick, and his son Sir Ralph, supporting the Earl of Hertford's army which was laying waste the Scottish borders:

> cam and mett at a tower on the Marse called Hutton Hall, belonging to John Hume, seased, burned the Hall, and so cam doon the Whitadder where there is very strange coves in crags and quarrels: these wan the said coves and slew in tow of them that was holden IX or X men and take in the other caves that gave over Xii prisoners whereof divers of them was very sore hurt.

About 1640 the Homes sold Hutton to the Johnston family in whose possession it remained for nearly two centuries. In 1876 it passed to Sir Dudley Coutts Marjoribanks, afterwards first Baron Tweedmouth. At that time it still remained a picturesque and interesting building which had received no major alterations for three hundred years. The most ancient part is the square three-storey keep at the south-east angle, to which is attached a circular projecting turret containing the staircase. This *ensemble* dates from the fifteenth or early sixteenth centuries. In the late sixteenth century the building was greatly enlarged by the addition of an L-shaped extension on the west side of the keep. Over the principal entrance are the arms of the Home family, with the initials, now almost entirely obliterated, AH (for Alexander Home?) and EH (Elizabeth Home), and the date 1573 which had already disappeared by the late nineteenth century; it is probable that this is the date of the western extension. Internally, the ground floor of this structure was vaulted and comprised cellars and kitchen offices. On the first floor were the principal rooms. The west arm contained the drawing-room and was divided by wooden partitions. In the central block were two rooms joined by a screens passage; the western of the two had late seventeenth or early eighteenth-century wooden panelling and a fine fireplace with a triangular pediment supported by fluted columns. The second room was the most attractive in the entire edifice and retained its original late sixteenth-century oak panelling, stone fireplace and plaster ceiling which was decorated with roses and interlacing patterns. On the floor above were bedrooms.

Regrettably the attractive irregularity of the exterior, with its windows at different levels and sizes and steep-pitched roof and chimneys, was 'tidied up' by Lord Tweedmouth. By the time the Royal Commission for Scotland on Ancient and Historical Monuments came to survey Hutton in 1908, instead of something with the character of Traquair House near Peebles, a Border residence which Hutton resembled, it had become a rather bland rich man's residence. Lord Tweedmouth removed the pitched roof over the central portion and

Hutton Castle just before Burrell purchased it.

Hutton Castle in the 1950's

added another storey for bedrooms. He also modified the roof-line of the western arm and introduced a battlemented parapet to the entire building. Further modifications included the heightening of the circular staircase turret adjoining the original keep and the addition of a smaller pepperbox turret at the north-west angle. The other major alteration to the exterior was the construction of a low extension containing domestic offices which linked the north side of the keep with the east end of the main body of the house. Around the house, which

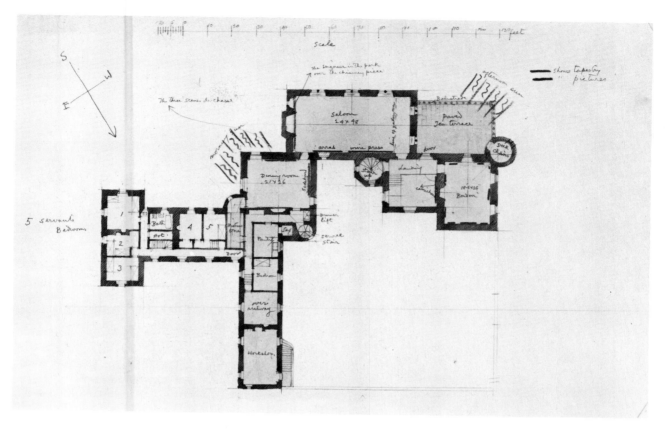

Plan of the first floor of Lorimer's initial proposal for a new house at Hutton, made in February 1916. Several tapestries are located. (Royal Commission on the Ancient and Historical Monuments of Scotland)

was covered in ivy, about four acres of gardens were laid out with a gravel drive providing access.

This, then, was the building and surroundings of which Burrell became the owner early in 1916. Even before he acquired it Burrell had sought the guidance of his old friend Robert Lorimer. The coolness that had arisen over Lorimer's remodelling of Great Western Terrace did not last long and the two men had continued to meet, often over luncheon, in the intervening years. Burrell, however, was neither of an easily forgiving nor forgetting nature and taking into account the strong personalities of both men it was with hindsight a serious error of judgement on Lorimer's part to become involved. In October 1915 he made a survey of Hutton, which included correspondence with at least one of the firms which had carried out work for Lord Tweedmouth, and in February of the following year he made a plan of the existing structure. From the outset Lorimer concluded that Hutton was quite unsuitable as a residence for Burrell. In the same month he drew up plans for an entirely new three-storeyed house on the site. It was on the grand scale of Formakin in Renfrewshire, which Lorimer had recently built for John A. Holms, the Glaswegian stock-broker who had been his best man, and closely resembled it in layout and Scottish baronial features. The designs were so detailed that paintings and tapestries are located, and several of the latter are even named. To Lorimer's disappointment Burrell did not greet his proposals with much enthusiasm. Lorimer then suggested that Burrell should occupy the house as it stood, merely whitewashing a few rooms, for the duration of the war so that he could familiarise himself with it and make up his mind about his future requirements. The advice was sound, but not entirely disinterested. He hoped that Burrell would discover for himself the drawbacks of the house and would change his mind. Lorimer must have borne in mind Burrell's early enthusiasm for the possibilities of Newark Castle near St Monans and thought that now the sale of Burrell and Son's fleet was in full swing there could not be any financial restraints. Lorimer, of course, had much to gain by convincing his old friend of the desirability of a residence on the scale of that of Burrell's rival collector Holms, especially as his country-house work, which was the mainstay of his practice, had declined since the outbreak of the war.

Burrell, however, declined Lorimer's advice and did not move in. Early in May he wrote to Lorimer from the Marine Hotel, Troon, where he and his wife were staying. Lorimer had meanwhile made suggestions for altering the existing buildings at Hutton, and these were greeted with enthusiasm. Lorimer's proposals included converting the ground floor rooms in the western arm, comprising the 'pug's parlour', butler's bedroom and butler's pantry, into an entrance hall, and installing central heating throughout the building. Burrell himself was full of ideas and, typically, took great interest in details. He asked for a plan showing the locations of all lights and their sockets, specified oak floors for the principal rooms and wanted the existing principal wooden staircase replaced by a stone one. He also suggested reducing the three bedrooms in the western arm to two and modifying Tweedmouth's domestic offices to provide accommodation for seven maids. In the same letter he reveals that he had decided either to sell Great Western Terrace or at best, only use it occasionally:

> How would it do to take the floor, oak panelling and fireplace of 8 GWT & use them in the entrance hall at Hutton? We shall eventually live at Hutton all the year round or nearly.

Burrell also told Lorimer that he and his wife wanted to replace the panelling in the dining room at Hutton with the linenfold dado from Great Western Terrace.

Immediately after posting this letter Burrell had second, more grandiose, thoughts and later the same day wrote again. This time he asked Lorimer to investigate whether it would be feasible to double the width of the western wing at Hutton. As the sketch which Burrell made in the letter shows, the intention was to provide more space for tapestries. He envisaged a hall on the ground floor for this purpose, supplementing

the existing drawing-room. He wanted the alterations to be done immediately in order to avoid a second upheaval later on.

The amicable tone of these two letters (the first was signed 'Yours sincerely', the second 'Yours very truly') was not maintained for long and the next one, which was written on 20 May, was in very different vein. It was occasioned by Lorimer's second attempt to interest Burrell in a much larger house, encouraged by Burrell's desire for more wall-space for the tapestries. The scheme proposed was an adaptation of that drawn up in February. This time, instead of demolishing completely the existing house, Lorimer retained the original keep. The remainder, i.e. the late sixteenth-century additions, was to be replaced by a forecourt overlooking the Whitadder; the new buildings, much more extensive and grander in scale and detail, were set further to the south and were linked to the old keep by a service wing. The entire design made much more of the natural beauties of the site, not only by providing a breath-taking view from the forecourt but also by replacing the existing approach road, which was set back from the Whitadder, by one which was situated much nearer the river and ran between it and the north face of the keep. It was an imaginative scheme and one which if it lacked the dramatic possibilities afforded by Newark Castle, would

South-west elevation of Lorimer's second design, with the old tower on the right. (Royal Commission on the Ancient and Historical Monuments of Scotland)

have given Burrell a residence on a scale commensurate with his ever-growing collection.

In the event, Lorimer's suggestions back-fired with disastrous consequences. His scheme was expensive and he chose the wrong moment to press it. The duration and eventual outcome of the war were unpredictable and the sale of Burrell and Son's ships was by no means complete. These were considerations which must have reinforced Burrell's in-built abhorrence of heavy spending. His reaction was tart. Not only did he reject the idea utterly, it also caused him to shelve any substantial alterations to the existing fabric:

> . . . as I informed you I am quite happy with the exterior of Hutton as it stands and I am not prepared to remove any part of it. All I thought of doing was what I indicated in my letters of 7 instant but since writing them I have decided to do only the undermentioned, leaving the rest for consideration after the war is over.

The works listed are relatively minor and included the earlier proposal to make an entrance hall in the ground floor of the western arm, but to leave the drawing-room and wooden staircase as they were. How trifling these alterations were can be gauged from his concluding remark:

> We should like to get into the house as early as possible and should be glad if the work can be completed by the middle or end of July.

Burrell signed the letter 'Yours faithfully', an indication of the coolness that had developed once more between the two old friends.

Within three weeks of writing this letter Burrell and his wife, who were still staying at the Marine Hotel, were considering enlarging the domestic wing built by Lord Tweedmouth. On 6 June Burrell wrote to Lorimer enclosing a sketch of this extension. It was to be of two storeys and include bedrooms for six maids and two male servants in addition to various other rooms. At the end of June Burrell called at Lorimer's office in Edinburgh to go over the plans drawn up by Lorimer both for the extension and for the removal of the stone vaults on the ground floor. Even these were too lavish and resulted in a bitter exchange of correspondence. Lorimer wrote to Burrell at the Oatlands Park Hotel, Weybridge (Surrey), and although his letter has not survived its gist is contained in Burrell's reply, dated four days later:

> If the words 'works that you have quite definitely determined to put through' refers to anything in the plans you handed me last week I wish to say that you are under a misapprehension. What I did was to promise to show to Connie the plans you proposed . . . we have decided not to adopt any of the suggestions made therein but to adhere to what I wrote you on 5 June – provided the work can be done at a moderate price.

Burrell added a slightly amended version of his sketch of the servants' wing, this time providing accommodation for housekeeper, cook, five maids and two men. He stipulated that its roof must be flat and its length should not exceed 35 feet, and repeated various earlier suggestions; for some extraordinary reason he proposed thinning certain walls. Relations between Burrell and Lorimer seem to have improved slightly for a while after this because the former's next letter, of 24 July, if business-like in tone and revealing his worries about costs did at least avoid recriminations. Burrell, however, fell into the error of seeing internal modifications in piece-meal fashion at the expense of the overall coherence of the scheme. His over-concern with detail must have made Lorimer's task very difficult and this, coupled with his chagrin at failing to interest Burrell in a grandiose project, caused him to write a letter which elicited a furious response from his client:

> . . . you write 'owing to the fact that no-one can teach you anything about your business you assume you are equally conversant with everything else'. I think this remark is surely unnecessary. What I have done is to decline your £40,000 proposals of which up till now I have received three although I made it clear from the beginning that I was quite pleased with the exterior and was not prepared to remov [sic] any part of the exterior – that all I wanted was to remove some of the partitions etc. in order to get more space inside and larger rooms and – provided the expense was not too much – to build some servants rooms at the east end of the house.

Burrell requested a sight of a new plan prepared by Lorimer:

> I hope it does not embody more than I wish.

In his next letter to Lorimer, written on 15 August from the Tinto Hotel, Symington in Lanarkshire, Burrell included yet another sketch plan of the servants' wing showing minor internal amendments. He reiterated his insistence on a flat roof in order not to dwarf the old tower. Once again his concerns about costs were well to the fore:

> Until we get estimates I do not wish anything outside of the present back door to be touched as, if the estimates are too high, we might decide to do no building until after the war is over.

By this time or very soon after there were men on site. On 24 August Shirran, the Clerk of Works, reported to Lorimer on a visit by Burrell during which he had issued direct instructions without consulting his architect:

> He insists on thinning the two kitchen walls and he wont allow the opening to [the] Service Stair to be built up. . . . We may manage to keep the men going for another fortnight but if nothing more is settled by then, some of them will have to go.

In spite of all the difficulties, by the beginning of September Burrell approved the construction of the servants' wing at a total price of £3,000:

> The figure, as you say, is very high but I have agreed to your [i.e. Lorimer's] suggestion that the wing be built now. . . . I rely upon your kindly seeing that the cost is kept within the amount named.

Although hampered by the variations insisted upon by Burrell on his visits to Hutton, work proceeded throughout September and October. On 28 October he wrote to Lorimer:

> . . . as the Maids Wing is going on so quickly we shall have plans drawn out for the rest of the house in case we decide to take in offers for it before the war is over.

There followed a long list of instructions regarding internal alterations, many of which do not differ from those proposed in May, and included having the main door placed in the south wall of the western arm. It was the impracticality of this and other features that precipitated another row. Early in November Lorimer, utterly exasperated, drafted a letter to Burrell in a tone quite alien to normal architect–client correspondence:

> . . . your proposal is to stop the principal corkscrew staircase at the Drawing room level and leave the bath room above more or less as it is. The upper floors would then solely be served by two extremely narrow corkscrew stairs – the one in the old tower being about as bad and difficult a one as I have ever seen, and the other a little if any better. As I have lived for nearly 40 years in a house entirely served by corkscrew stairs I am doubtless the last person who ought to know something about them from the practical point of view. At Kellie [at that time the summer residence in Fife of the Lorimer family, now owned by the National Trust for Scotland] there are four corkscrew stairs . . . when everyone is 'merry and bright' these stairs answer well enough but when anyone is not too strong . . . these stairs are a terrible trial [these last two words are crossed out]. I cannot picture to you the agony of trying to get my mother up and down the Turret stair to her bedroom the last year or two at Kellie. . . . I pointed out to you a central ideal place on the plans for introducing an automatic push button lifts [sic]. Although I have no expectation of you being influenced by my recommendation I wish to put it in black and white and in the plainest language that you will will be making a great mistake if you depend entirely on these two small cramped corkscrew stairs.

Burrell's letter had crossed with Lorimer's design, closely based on the front door at Stenhouse Mills, for the main entrance at Hutton and now the architect expressed himself forcibly on Burrell's ideas regarding its position and that of the cloakroom.

> From the practical point of view the door on the East, without a proper inner vestibule, is only a few points less bad than having it on the South. . . . Here again I have the experience of nearly 40 years at Kellie as a guide. . . . From lack of experience in dealing with these problems, you allow your ideas to be too much governed by what exists.

This last sentence is crossed out and replaced by the following:

> It is one of the A' B' C's of planning that a country house s^d have an outer hall with outer & inner door at *right angles* to each other &

so that in a windy day the servant shuts the inner door before she opens the outer one, all this & a convenient arrangement of cloakroom immediately adjoining the outer hall was shown on the recent plan I submitted to you & to which you – owing to your inability to benefit by the experience of other people – would not give even a moments consideration & you are going to live in the house & not me, & I must leave you to enjoy the very untidyest arrangement you are insistent on & also the joy of walking the full length of your hall & its brass dishes & coat armour, before you reach your cloakroom & get out of your wet waterproofs & umbrella.

Fortunately Lorimer did not send this letter, although in the end it would not have made any difference if he had. The stairs were to prove as impractical as Lorimer predicted. As Burrell and his wife reached old age they found it difficult to manage them. In the winter of 1948 he had a fall on one of the staircases and soon after the lift which Lorimer had advocated was at last installed. No-one but himself and Lady Burrell was permitted to use this lift. Before going away from Hutton he would switch off the electricity supply to the lift in order to enforce the ban.

Notwithstanding the bad feeling that had arisen between the two former friends work continued on the new wing until September 1917. The bills which were presented then led to further recriminations. There was an agreement that the costs of the alterations to the existing fabric and of the new wing should be kept separately, but owing to Burrell's constant site interference and instructions this had proved impossible; more seriously they had resulted in a considerable increase in overall expenditure. Burrell unfairly blamed Lorimer:

Had I known that it would have cost more I would never have allowed the work to go on. . . . Now you tell me you cannot say what the wing has cost. . . . Please let me have the surveyors figures as well as estimates for finishing the work in the wing which has still to be done.

Lorimer in turn accused Burrell of responsibility for the increase, and this caused the latter to make the final break:

It is true that you advised me to go into the house as it was for a time and that advice followed your earlier advice to knock down and remove the house and allow you to build a new one in its place as you considered that in its existing state the house was absolutely unworkable and impossible. But the fact that I did not choose to go into the house as it was is no reason why your repeated assurances that the wing could be carried out complete at £3000 or a little over should be so enormously exceeded.

The result is so unsatisfactory and annoying that I shall not require further professional assistance from you.

Lorimer made a last effort to retrieve the situation. On 29 October he wrote to Burrell explaining that the bad weather and the war made it very difficult to estimate building costs accurately; also that, as he had said to him on many occasions:

> . . . the type of work you insisted on doing in the old house, thinning walls, clearing out heavy vaults, enormous masses of masonry in chimneys, forming heating ducts, etc., was always expensive, and that when done there was little apparent value for the expenditure.

The letter concludes:

> . . . if I cease to act for you professionally, the loss will not be all on my own side. You will not easily find anyone who understands your stuff and the architectural setting it requires as I do.
>
> I shall regret, however, if a friendship of nearly twenty years' standing – which included some of the pleasantest experiences I have ever had – was to be brought to an equally abrupt conclusion.

This conciliatory tone failed to evoke a response from Burrell. Lorimer's involvement with Hutton and his friendship with Burrell had come to an end. Thirty years later Burrell still retained bitter memories of Lorimer's work at Hutton.

After the termination of Lorimer's commission nothing seems to have been done at Hutton for several years and the house was shut up. Although 8 Great Western Terrace remained in his possession Burrell preferred to live in a series of rented country properties, including Kilduff House near Haddington in Lothian, which he occupied from early 1917; in 1924 he moved to Broxmouth Park, just east of Dunbar. Both are eighteenth-century houses with substantial Victorian modifications and both were close enough to the railway to allow Burrell easy access to Hutton and to travel to London with a minimum of inconvenience.

Some time after the end of the First World War alterations to Hutton Castle began again. In view of the not-so-distant past history of the project Burrell's choice of one of Lorimer's pupils, Reginald Fairlie, as architect is surprising. Precisely for what Fairlie was responsible is uncertain, but he seems to have concentrated mainly on internal and external modifications to the western arm. These included the siting of the main entrance door in exactly the position Lorimer advised against; its detailing is far more mundane than that envisaged by Lorimer. One of Burrell's main concerns was the provision of new windows in the drawing-room and hall for the medieval stained glass he had recently acquired. In 1918 the outstanding collection formed by Sir William Jerningham and displayed in his chapel at Costessey Hall in Norfolk had been bought by Grosvenor Thomas. Soon after it was exhibited in his house in Hyndland, Glasgow, and Burrell immediately made a number of purchases, including an important three-light window with scenes from the life of St John the Evangelist and part of a Tree of Jesse,

*13 ANNUNCIATION by a Dutch
painter known as the Master of the
Brunswick Diptych; one of the
15th-century treasures in the
Collection.*

14 *Detail of the Tudor oak panelling
from Harrington Hall, with which
Burrell decorated his dining room at
Hutton Castle.*

15 JOCKEYS IN THE RAIN *by Degas,
whose paintings Burrell bought
regularly between the two wars.*

16 *A remarkable bargain: the armorial
table carpet apparently woven for the
widow of Sir Andrew Luttrell in
about 1544. Burrell paid £3,100 for
it in 1928. Six years earlier it had
fetched £5,565.*

17 Late 17th-century needlework box embroidered with silk which Burrell bought from Frank Partridge in 1934.

19 The rare Romanesque bronze known as the TEMPLE PYX which Burrell was persuaded to buy by the Hunts, who told him that if he did not it would be sold to an American collector or museum.

18 The stained-glass panel depicting Beatrix van Valkenburg whose tenuous links with Hutton Castle so excited Burrell.

20 Another great bargain: the stained-glass panel depicting the prophet Jeremiah (detail seen here). When Burrell acquired it in 1923 for £114 5s 10d, it was not recognized as forming part of the glazing of the Abbey of St Denis, which was carried out in 1140–45. The panel is one of the earliest surviving examples of European figural window glass.

21 The only Gauguin in the Collection: a chalk drawing of a Breton girl.

22 *Le Meunier, son Fils et L'Ane* by Honoré Daumier, for which Burrell paid £8,000 in 1926. It was his most expensive picture up to that time.

both painted for Rouen churches in the early sixteenth century. These and other panels demanded an architectural setting on a scale beyond that of the existing window openings at Hutton. While the new ones were being made Burrell loaned the ancient glass to the Victoria and Albert Museum. In the event it was to be another nine years before he was to see the panels in place, not least because once again he fell out with his architect. The cause of the break is unknown; many years later Burrell said that Fairlie made several serious blunders, but did not specify them. It seems, though, that the fabric of Hutton was substantially complete when Fairlie departed the scene in the early 1920's.

After the expenditure of so much effort and the incurring of so much bad feeling the house remained what it had been since Lord Tweedmouth's alterations, an undistinguished grouping of disparate elements. Moreover what remained of its interior character at the time Burrell purchased it had now been lost by his insistence on the removal of the ground floor vaulting. At the end of the day Lorimer's judgement is vindicated. It was a case of the wrong house, maybe even the wrong site. It suffers especially by comparison with Lorimer's plans for Newark Castle and his suggestions for a much grander residence at Hutton. In his heart of hearts Burrell may have recognised the drawbacks of Hutton, but if so he was not the man to admit publicly to a mistake. In any case he was not prepared to spend the amount of money such schemes required and that was that. He may even have been justified in his shunning of such an outlay. Certainly the lavish building projects of two fellow-collectors contributed to their financial problems. Holms ran into difficulties before Formakin could be completed and the crippling costs of William Randolph Hearst's Californian palace complex at San Simeon and his castle at St Donat's in Wales were major factors which led to the crisis in his finances in 1937 and the subsequent dispersal of large parts of his collection. It is estimated that San Simeon alone cost Hearst between thirty and forty million dollars to build and $6,000 per day to maintain when guests were in residence. The annual upkeep of St Donat's, the modernisation of which entailed an expenditure of a trifling $1,250,000, amounted to $342,500: the total time Hearst actually occupied it was not more than four months. Burrell was to benefit from the financial embarrassment of both Hearst and Holms.

Whatever the architectural shortcomings of Hutton, they were at least partly redeemed by its contents. Since 1917 Burrell had been buying pictures, furniture, and *objets d'art* on an unprecedented scale. From the outset he was determined to make showpieces of the drawing room and hall, and to achieve this as well as arrange the other rooms he once more sought professional advice. This time he looked beyond the ranks of the architectural profession. At last he found two men who could cope with him. Indeed, with both of them he formed life-long friendships. The first was Wilfred Drake, a shy, likeable man whose father was a well-known Exeter glazier. Wilfred developed a deep love of stained glass and after the First World War he went into partnership with Grosvenor Thomas, for whom his brother Maurice compiled the catalogue of the Costessey Hall Collection. After Grosvenor Thomas' death in 1923 his son Roy, who was living in New York, took his place in the firm and handled the American side of the business. Burrell met Drake in the early days of his association with the elder Grosvenor Thomas and in 1927 he sought his advice in setting his collection up in the windows at Hutton.

The second person Burrell turned to played the more important rôle. Frank Surgey joined the well-known interior decorating firm of White Allom on leaving school and learned his trade on schemes which included Buckingham Palace. In his spare time he studied architecture at the Regent Street Polytechnic. The outbreak of war in 1914 found him in New York, working as Sir Charles Allom's assistant on the decoration of the ruthless steel magnate Henry Clay Frick's mansion at 70th Street and Fifth Avenue. The scheme was carried out in collaboration with Duveen, who granted Frick the privilege of becoming one of his most favoured clients. Allom, incidentally, was to carry out the modernisation of St Donat's for Hearst. At the end of the war Surgey returned to England and began on his own account to advise on the restoration of old houses. So successful was this venture that around 1920 he left White Allom and started his own firm; a few years later he was joined by the flamboyant extrovert Murray Adams-Acton, another former employee of White Allom, and together they formed Acton Surgey Ltd, specialising in architectural renovation and interior decoration, including the provision of antique furniture and fittings. Burrell's first purchases from Frank Surgey were made at the beginning of

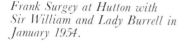

Frank Surgey at Hutton with Sir William and Lady Burrell in January 1954.

1925 and he formed such a high regard for his abilities that within a few months he entrusted him with the task of completing Hutton Castle.

Surgey's brief was the total re-furbishment of the interior of the building. This was not confined to fittings such as curtains and lights as well as antique furniture, etc., but included the provision of huge stone fireplaces and chimneypieces, doors and panelling. In stark contrast with Burrell's reluctance to spend money on the fabric, there was no penny-pinching with the interior. The scheme got under way early in 1926, when Burrell purchased Late Gothic stone and oak fireplaces and doors for the principal bedrooms, in addition to much furniture. Two important acquisitions were a large stone chimneypiece for the drawing room and a complete room of Early Tudor elaborately carved oak panelling from Harrington Hall in Lincolnshire and another stone fireplace; the panelling and fireplace, which cost Burrell the large sum of £4,500, were intended for the dining room; attractive as this *ensemble* was it can only be described as a mixed blessing, for it entailed the removal and disposal of the *in situ* late sixteenth-century panelling of the room together with the plaster ceiling, thereby completing the loss of the original interior of the house. None of these items was delivered at Hutton for the time being, no doubt because of necessary internal modifications. Burrell must have hoped to see the house completed speedily, and it was sufficiently advanced by the summer of 1927 for him, Lady Burrell and their daughter to move in at last, more than eleven years after the purchase of the property. Late in the year, however, yet another delay was caused by the need to take up all the floors as they were of unseasoned wood (the responsibility for this was presumably laid at Fairlie's door).

See plate 14

A year which had begun so well for Burrell with the announcement in the New Years Honours List of his knighthood for his services to art in Scotland and public works thus ended on a sour note. It was also a year marred by family tragedy, for his brother George died in September on a fishing holiday in Northern Ireland.

Early in 1928 the fireplaces and panelling were delivered and installed, as were a stone image bracket for the hall and a late twelfth-century corbel table which was set up in the adjoining vestibule. In April Burrell turned his attention to the setting-up of his stained glass collection in the windows and recalled the Rouen Jesse and St John the Evangelist panels from the Victoria and Albert Museum. Wilfred Drake came up to advise and by the end of June the St John glass was in place in the large three-light window in the drawing room. The other windows in this room were completed by 21 July and the rest of the ancient glass was distributed throughout the house, including the hall, the bedrooms and even the servants' pantry: for this last room Burrell had such a low opinion of the servants' sense of responsibility that he

The dining room at Hutton Castle in 1915

The dining room as reconstructed by Burrell and Frank Surgey

asked Drake to send him a plain sheet to protect the medieval panel. On 18 December 1929 Burrell reported to Drake that his entire collection of two hundred and twenty-two panels was installed, and the latter subsequently made a room-by-room catalogue.

While the stained glass was in progress, the fitting-out of the principal rooms with pelmets, light fittings and doors proceeded under Frank Surgey's direction. Once again, Burrell's changes of mind seem to have hampered things and added to the cost. For example he decided to extend the dining room panelling, with the apparent aim of allowing tapestries to be set up; this involved Surgey in dismantling the already erected panelling from Harrington Hall and finding some original linenfold panels, matching them and setting the *ensemble* up again. This work alone cost £943.

The scheme was finally completed early in 1932. Its scale and quality were reflected in the final accounts submitted by Acton Surgey. The quantities were staggering: no fewer than eight fifteenth/early sixteenth-century oak clavels and stone jambs for fireplaces and three medieval stone chimneypieces. Some 42 oak doors were supplied, some of which dated back to the Middle Ages whilst others were more recent. The cost of restoring and adapting 36 of them amounted to the considerable total of £408 10s. In addition Frank Surgey had 21 oak radiator fronts and 13 pelmets specially carved in a Gothic-cum-Early Renaissance style to blend with Burrell's furniture and fittings: the four pelmets for the dining room cost £147, the six for the hall and vestibule £192. A major item of expense was 22 wrought-iron chandeliers; that on the landing of the new servants' wing was copied from one in the Victoria and Albert Museum. The total expenditure on the chandeliers was £1,024 10s, the dearest being a pair for the drawing-room.

Even the sums spent on chandeliers were exceeded by the cost of the

Lady Burrell's bedroom

soft fittings, comprising curtains, window-seats, light-shades, and valances for the beds and carpets. They were all supplied by leading specialist firms, mainly from the West End of London. The velvet for the curtains and light-shades alone cost just under £2,000 and a special spread loom was installed to make them up. The total came to the huge sum of £4,254 15s 7d, including Acton Surgey's commission. The quality of the curtains, window-seats and light-shades is attested by their survival in such good condition today, where they can be seen in the reconstructed Hutton rooms in the Burrell Collection building. It was with understandable hyperbole that Burrell claimed many years later that they were the finest ever made.

Total payments to Acton Surgey Ltd for fittings and for numerous items of furniture, tapestries and sculpture amounted to £57,846 16s 8d. And this did not take into account many other acquisitions, including arms and armour, stained glass, tapestries, rugs and carpets which Burrell had been collecting from other sources since he had acquired Hutton.

The country gentleman: Burrell (mounted) at a shooting party with Lord Digby on the 'glorious 12th' in 1936. (Glasgow Herald)

Once settled at Hutton Burrell was able to live the life of a leisured country gentleman, entertaining shooting parties: in November 1927 he acquired a Purdey shotgun for this purpose. He also played the part of the wealthy aesthete, showing his treasures to distinguished visitors and guests. To maintain the house with its valuable contents and the estate demanded a large staff and here as with the internal refurbishment Burrell did not stint himself. From the beginning he envisaged a domestic establishment much larger than that employed by Lord Tweedmouth, hence the construction of the new wing. A housemaid at Hutton in the period 1927–30 recalls that the living-in staff consisted of the following: cook/housekeeper, butler, footman (who wore a green livery with yellow facings), lady's maid, two housemaids, kitchen maid, scullery maid and between-maid. The outside staff numbered about eight, including a head gardener, gamekeeper and chauffeur. The Burrells were very concerned that the grounds should be properly maintained. Well into the 1950's, when the house was being run down, the lawns and flower-beds remained immaculate. The 'below stairs' staff worked the customary long hours and the wages were not exactly lavish: the housemaid received £4 6s 8d a month in addition to her keep, out of which she had to buy and maintain her two uniforms (a print dress with white apron for the morning, a black dress with white apron for the afternoon), but this was also standard practice. In accommodation and facilities provided, such as hot and cold running water in the rooms, the servants at Hutton enjoyed above-average working conditions.

Life in the years down to the Second World War seems to have been

No 1 bedroom

agreeable enough for Burrell's employees. There were the usual petty jealousies and rivalries, and touches of humour were provided by the efforts – unsuccessful – of the butler and footman to teach the resident parrot to swear. Burrell himself was approachable and straightforward in his dealings with the staff, although a stickler for seeing that their duties were performed properly. This occasionally led to friction, such as when he insisted that the countless grooves and carved surfaces of an elaborate four-poster bed should be cleaned with matchsticks. Burrell does not always seem to have understood the priorities of the less fortunate classes. He couldn't comprehend why a cook wanted to leave when she could enjoy medieval stained glass in the windows of her bedroom. Moreover his obsession with security over some rooms, particularly the drawing-room, created difficulties for the servants. He kept them locked for long periods, which meant that when the domestics did gain access for cleaning there was far more work to be done. Nor was access to the drawing-room restricted just for the servants; even close relatives felt that it was like a museum and they were not allowed to sit in the chairs for fear of damaging them.

Security was not Burrell's only concern. His anxiety to avoid what he considered to be unnecessary expense was also well to the fore. If a gardener broke a spade he had to take it to the master and explain the circumstances; he would then receive a lecture on thrift. In Burrell's bedroom was placed the master-switch for the electricity supply throughout the building. When he retired for the night he was in the habit of throwing this switch, plunging the Castle into darkness regardless of whether the other residents were still up, reading or whatever. One regular visitor records that this used to happen at 10 p.m. sharp. Furthermore, as Lord Clark relates, Burrell's obsession with the cost of electricity was carried to such an extreme that he carried a key which unlocked boxes encasing the light switches in every room. Even members of the family had to come to him for this key. In this as well as in other small economies Burrell practised the old adage that if you look after the pennies the pounds would take care of themselves. He is still remembered in the antique-dealing firm of Frank Partridge and Sons as being extremely brief when he made telephone calls. 'Ring me back later,' he would say and hurriedly put the receiver down. He was much more long-winded when the other party paid the bill.

In other respects guests were well provided for. They were surrounded by antique furniture, in the windows was medieval stained glass, and on the floors were valuable oriental rugs. Lord Clark remembered one visit:

> When we first entered our bedroom at Hatton [sic] I said 'That's a fine rug, Sir William.' 'Aye, but you'll find a better one underneath.' There was, and I said so. 'Aye, but the one under that there's a better one still,' and so forth for five deep.

Clark's memory was not entirely accurate, for only in the drawing-room were any carpets piled one on top of the other.

Of the many guests at Hutton, dealers, collectors, family friends, none can have pleased Burrell more than Queen Mary. A lover of antiques herself she came for tea at Hutton Castle early in September 1930, accompanied by an aristocratic entourage. The re-furbishing of the house was not quite complete, but she must have been impressed with what she saw. For years after the Queen's visit Burrell flew the Scottish saltire from the flagstaff at Hutton on her birthday. What was visible at Hutton in 1930 did not represent the entire range of Burrell's collecting activities to date, nor was his hunger for new acquisitions in any way confined by the limited space available in the Castle.

5

BETWEEN THE WARS

He was not simply an amasser; he was an aesthete.
Lord Clark on Burrell

VEN before he had achieved his ambition to live in baronial surroundings at Hutton, Burrell and his wife travelled in England and abroad frequently. In 1921 and 1922 they wintered at Cannes and in the following year they went on a cruise to the Far East, calling at Calcutta, Agra and Rangoon. At Calcutta Sir William purchased for Lady Burrell an emerald pendant for the large sum of £700. The pattern of travelling was not broken by the occupation of Hutton in 1927; if anything the tempo increased. From 1934 until the outbreak of the Second World War they spent the winter months in Jamaica. Burrell missed these cruises badly during the war and longed for their resumption, although in the event it was not to be. There is no evidence that he ever visited the United States, which is curious in the light of his interests, coinciding as they did with those of a number of American collectors. Apart from his Jamaican cruises and the Far East journey in 1922–23 he confined himself to Europe and England. He was a constant visitor to both London and Paris; the latter city he went to at least once a year, usually in the spring or summer, between the World Wars. In England the Burrells were also fond of Nantwich and Bournemouth and spent a number of holidays in both places. On the Continent they spent a considerable amount of time taking the waters at the fashionable spa resorts of Badgastein in the Austrian Alps, Evian-les-Bains on the Lake of Geneva and Bagnoles-de-l'Orne in Normandy, to alleviate the phlebitis from which Lady Burrell suffered. Sometimes they went further afield, as in 1933 when they visited Spain and Madeira. Although they stayed in the best hotels (in London they favoured

Claridge's) the itineraries must have been very taxing, particularly as neither of them was in the first flush of youth (Burrell in 1931 was already seventy years old) and Lady Burrell was never in robust health. In the period June–August 1930 Burrell went to Vienna, where he attended the auction of the renowned Figdor Collection, Munich and Paris. In 1932 the Burrells undertook even more punishing travels and were absent from Hutton for eight months.

Some of Burrell's journeys were necessitated by public duties. From 1923 until 1946 his Trusteeship of the National Galleries of Scotland demanded his presence in Edinburgh, and for seven years from September 1927 he was a Trustee of the National Gallery of British Art (now the Tate Gallery) and attended Board meetings whenever he could. But by far and away his main motive in travelling was his love of art. Wherever Burrell went he viewed as much as possible, in public museums and galleries, special exhibitions, in situ in churches and houses. As was observed earlier, he was never one for learning from books and academic journals, as the dearth of serious art publications in his library reveals (there are certain exceptions, notably works on tapestries). This no doubt stemmed from his lack of an academic up-bringing, but between the wars he sought to rectify it by visual education; on at least two occasions this was the raison d'être for under-taking particular trips. In 1925 he wrote to Wilfred Drake asking for a list of parish churches and cathedrals in England where good stained glass could be found. When he got the list he replied to Drake:

> Of all the glass you tell me about I have only seen York Minster so that everything else will be new to me and I am consequently looking forward with great pleasure to seeing as much of it as I can. Of all the Arts I think Tapestry and stained glass are two of the most attractive. . . .

With his time up to the First World War occupied almost exclusively with business affairs his opportunities to experience much stained glass were limited, although it is perhaps a little surprising that he had seen so little of an art that appealed so much to him and of which he was already a collector of some standing. It is even more remarkable that as late as 1939 Drake had to provide a list of glass for him to see in the churches of Somerset and Devon, including Exeter Cathedral and Doddiscombsleigh.

It is typical of Burrell that he should consult a dealer rather than an academic specialist for advice on these tours. His non-university back-ground cut him off from the contacts with the scholarly world which he would otherwise have enjoyed, but his temperament and environment drew him naturally to those engaged in the commercial side of the art trade; in common with Arthur Kay his attitude was conditioned by his respect for the practical man of business and is put succinctly in a letter he wrote in 1953 to Andrew Hannah:

My experience is that a *good* dealer is more acute as a rule rather than a Professor. That is because the dealer if he makes a mistake has to pay, but the Professor has not and is less acute.

For this reason Burrell was always most at home in the salerooms of the leading auction houses and in the premises of dealers.

Although by 1914 Burrell had made some important acquisitions and had already largely determined the range of his interests, he was by international standards a collector of minor significance, far removed from the ranks of Henry Clay Frick, J. Pierpont Morgan and Henry Huntington in the United States, and even of the German collector of medieval art, Alexander Schnütgen (1843–1918). In the 1920's and 30's he emerged from his long apprenticeship and became one of Europe's leading collectors, if not quite on a par with Henry Walters of Baltimore (d. 1931), and the legendary William Randolph Hearst (1863–1951).

Burrell's rise to such exalted stature is even more worthy of note when it is remembered that although through the sale of the fleet and shrewd investments he had become a very wealthy man, he was not in the league of Walters or Hearst. The shy and modest Henry Walters, whom Burrell closely resembles in many respects, made a fortune from his Atlantic Coastline Railroad. The Croesus of all the inter-war collectors was Hearst, who in 1919 inherited the vast sum of eleven million dollars in addition to the $7,500,000 he had already received in 1895, and multiplied it over and over again. He is estimated to have spent on collecting alone some fifty million dollars, quite apart from his massive outlay on his estates at San Simeon and elsewhere. In so doing he over-reached himself, to Burrell's considerable benefit. This sum may be contrasted with the latter's scale of spending. Between 1911 and 1957, the period of the Purchase Books, he spent an average of £20,000 per year on works of art, although between the wars even this figure is inflated by some of the reproduction fittings for Hutton Castle and modern jewellery. His largest single outlay in any one year was £79,280, in 1936.

How then, did Burrell manage to advance to the forefront of collectors? The answer lies in a combination of his own visual perception, an amazing memory (an aptitude he had in common with Hearst) and his shrewd application of business methods learned in the hard school of the pre-1914 shipping world to the art market and those who made their living in it; to these assets may be added the peripheral one of personal frugality, an aspect of his character which has already been touched upon *vis-à-vis* Hutton Castle and which became more marked as the years went by. His spartan life-style was partly adopted for health reasons. Thus although he stayed at the best hotels he ate very sparingly. Frank Surgey always remembered a dinner with the Burrells at Claridge's at which Burrell ordered a full meal for Surgey and Lady Burrell and merely had porridge himself. Also present was that streak of stinginess and fear that everyone was after his money which runs through many wealthy people (the late J. Paul Getty is but the most recent example). Burrell abhorred the expense of taxis and when in London would always walk or take the Underground in order to save money. He was always on the look-out for the chance to save money when travelling further afield. Lord Clark related the following story:

> He discovered that there was an excursion ticket from Berwick to Dunkerque, via London. 'And would you believe it, the silly bodies have made the Dunkerque portion detachable.' In summer he always took this ticket, sold the Dunkerque portion, and got to London for perhaps the price of a pound less than the price of a normal ticket. He used to describe this manoeuvre with particular glee.

He was very resentful when he had to spend more money on travel than he wanted to. Returning from one of his West Indies cruises he told Tom Honeyman, then working for the firm of Alex Reid and Lefevre in London, that a friend of Honeyman's had been on the same ship:

> He must have been very well off. He had a suite de-luxe – I can't afford that, but I have always got to have a separate cabin on a ship or a room in a hotel because, you see, I snore! Let me tell you, Honeyman, that snore has cost me thousands of pounds.

This side of Burrell's character is the best remembered today, but it should be borne in mind that most of the stories concerning his penny-pinching date from the last decade of his life and it should not be wondered at if a man in his nineties developed particular obsessions. Moreover, he was also capable of generosity towards those whom he trusted and served him well. On several occasions between the wars Wilfred Drake and Tom Honeyman received presents of game from shoots at Hutton and in 1940 Burrell gave the latter a picture by Leslie Hunter, an artist Honeyman particularly admired. In business matters none of the dealers had any difficulties with payments from him; he almost invariably paid promptly in cash and did not ask for credit. On at least two occasions Burrell paid Drake sums in excess of those which he had been charged. In 1939 Drake even wrote to thank Burrell and his wife for their 'liberal kindness and generosity'. Burrell's parsimony in his private life extended to his art collecting; he always avoided spending a pound when a penny would do. Although this attitude was ingrained in him, to some extent it was in the years between the World Wars dictated by force of circumstances. His resources were by American standards comparatively limited and in order to compete he had to make the most of what he did have available.

In some respects Burrell was fortunate in that he was buying in a buyer's market. The previous generation of fabulously wealthy American collectors, like J. Pierpont Morgan and Henry Clay Frick, were no longer around and Burrell's own transatlantic contemporaries (and the art market as a whole) were affected by the world recession of 1929–33. The exception was Hearst who continued to pay inflated prices until his personal crash came in 1937. Even when the recovery began in 1933 the market remained poor and some areas which had been much sought after during the 1920's, notably English eighteenth-century portraiture, French Barbizon School painting and even the works of Degas, never regained their former buoyancy until long after the Second World War. In the case of artists like Lawrence, Reynolds, Romney and Raeburn the market has never recovered, notwithstanding Joseph Duveen's efforts in the late 1930's to support his own prices. The decorative and applied arts were perhaps less affected. English sixteenth-century oak furniture and the best medieval tapestries remained in demand in the United States, although the latter were beginning to fall out of favour as most wealthy collectors now preferred easily-maintained apartments to the large mansions with acres of wall-space favoured by the pre-First World War generations. Generally speaking the best objects always made money, but even so the art market was not in a healthy state. Silver in particular was badly hit in the 1930's by the fall in its bullion value and the later Chinese porcelains, the *famille noire* and *famille jaune* wares popular with American millionaires during the First World War, lost much ground in the same period. The London salerooms were particularly depressed between 1931 and 1935. A.C.R. Carter in *The Year's Art* for 1932 said it was the worst year he could remember in the saleroom since he began records in the early 1880's.

It is against this background of declining prices and a sluggish market that Burrell's collecting policies in the 1920's and 1930's must be seen. His money could go further than it would have done had he been collecting before the First World War on the scale upon which he now embarked; but even so it took careful managing. It can hardly be coincidental that with the exception of 1931, his expenditure rose as the depression deepened. The totals for the years from 1919 until the outbreak of the Second World War are as follows:

1919 £16,451	1926 £33,567	1933 £40,291
1920 £15,724	1927 £40,816	1934 £35,216
1921 £7,702	1928 £41,142	1935 £26,712
1922 £10,378	1929 £44,359	1936 £79,280
1923 £23,098	1930 £36,365	1937 £53,609
1924 £14,934	1931 £10,866	1938 £41,147
1925 £27,648	1932 £39,681	1939 £28,578

Furthermore, an examination of the Purchase Books for the same period suggests very strongly that what determined Burrell's selection of certain major fields of acquisition was the state of the market. This does not apply to the comparatively minor items (in terms of price) of English seventeenth and eighteenth-century furniture, silver, and table glass and Chinese Kangxi ceramics which make up the majority of his acquisitions between 1918 and 1939; it does, however, apply to paintings and tapestries, which in this period were consistently his most costly acquisitions. In the years 1917–21 he flirted briefly with an old flame, the eighteenth-century British portrait, but after making a few minor acquisitions (with the exception of Hogarth's *Mrs Anne Lloyd* *See plate 10* which cost him £800 in 1919) he left the field to the American clients of Duveen and the enormous prices they were charged: in 1921 Duveen sold Gainsborough's *Blue Boy* to Henry Huntington for £148,000, the story of which transaction is recounted splendidly in Behrman's biography of the art dealer. Instead Burrell in the 1920's turned his attention not only to other old favourites like Joseph Crawhall and the Hague and Barbizon School artists, but also committed himself wholeheartedly to Degas. In this it is possible to detect the guiding hand of Alex Reid, although by no means all of Burrell's purchases of works by this artist came from him. Around 1901 he had gingerly tested the water by acquiring *La Lorgneuse*, but it was not until 1917 that he added another Degas. Even then another four years were to elapse before a third joined the Collection, but from then onwards he purchased works by this artist almost every year until 1930, with a late flurry of additions in 1937; among these is the well-known *Jockeys in the* *See plate 15* *Rain*, bought at the sale of Leonard Gow's collection. On the whole the price of Degas' pictures remained on the low side between the wars, and never approached the £21,000 paid in 1913 for *Danseuses à la Barre* which is now in the Louvre. As late as 1940 the famous Paris art dealing firm of Durand-Ruel apparently had some of the larger ballet subjects still on their books for as little as £6,000 each. Degas appealed to Burrell very much. In 1949 he wrote: '. . . I am very sorry I never met him. Reid might have taken me to his studios had we been in Paris together but I was hardly ever in Paris at the same time as Reid.' The prices must also have been attractive; his dearest Degas, *La Repetition*, cost only £6,500 in 1926.

In the following year Burrell paid out his largest sum to date for a single work of art, £12,600, a figure which was not to be surpassed until 1948 (if the dealer's commission is excluded on the Rembrandt *Self-Portrait* for which he paid £12,500 in 1946). It was not for a picture, but a Franco-Burgundian tapestry of *c*.1450–75 known as *The Grape Harvest*. *See plate 3* He used to say that you got far more for your money if you bought tapestries, and in the late 1920's and 1930's he was consistently prepared to pay more for them than for paintings. As we have already seen, one of Burrell's first loves had been Late Gothic and Early Renaissance tapestries, but the revival of this interest was not perhaps unconnected with the modest prices for which they could now be obtained, compared with the astounding sums spent by J. Pierpont Morgan in the last few years of his life (Morgan is reputed to have paid Duveen £72,055 in 1902 for a single Flemish tapestry of c.1500, which formerly belonged to Cardinal Mazarin; according to Duveen the price was a mere £65,000) and those achieved in 1916 at the dispersal of his collection: two Brussels tapestries after Bernard van Orley for which Morgan had paid £12,000 in 1912 were bought by Duveen and sold by him to another rich American collector, Joseph Widener, for no less than £103,300. One can easily imagine Burrell shaking his head in horror at such figures, and they are likely to have been an important factor in deterring him from adding substantially to his collection at the time. After this, with the exception of the set of six Unicorn tapestries bought in 1923 by J.D. Rockefeller Jr for £245,000 and which are now in the Cloisters, New York, the market settled down and Burrell was able to make some remarkable bargains. To give but one example, in 1928 he acquired

See plate 16 from Acton Surgey the famous armorial table carpet apparently woven around 1544 for the widow of Sir Andrew Luttrell of Dunster in Somerset and which had descended for generations in the Edgecombe family of Cotehele in Cornwall. At £3,100 it was exceptionally good value, especially as it had been sold only six years earlier for £5,565.

The low prices Burrell generally paid reflect the lack of competition in the inter-war years, especially from British collectors. There were some, notably Sir Alan Barlow and Sir Percival David in the field of Chinese ceramics, bronzes and jades, and Dr Walter Hildburgh (d.1955) and Dr Philip Nelson (d.1953) for medieval art. Hildburgh specialised in English alabasters, all of which in 1946 he gave to the Victoria and Albert Museum. Alabasters also appealed to Nelson, who shared a similar background to Burrell in that his father was a Liverpool ship-owner, and in addition he had some fine sculpture and stained glass; in 1913 he published a scholarly account of English medieval glass-painting. Most of Burrell's rivals were across the Atlantic, but his financial handicap was offset both by his closer geographical location to the sources and his willingness to travel in search of additions to his collection; Burrell was not a man to sit back and select from what was put before him. Moreover his chief competitors gradually fell by the wayside. Henry Walters' wings were clipped by the Wall Street crash of 1929 and he died two years later, whereas Hearst ceased to be a threat from 1937, when his vast newspaper, landowning and mining empire teetered on the edge of bankruptcy and he was forced to sell two-thirds of his collection. Even with those whose interests seemed to coincide most closely with Burrell circumstances worked in his favour. Henry Walters and the Frankfurt businessman Robert von Hirsch shared his taste for medieval art, but within that field they had particular regard for the Romanesque period, for which Burrell did not care very much. Walters also formed a major collection of illuminated manuscripts and this was another aspect of medieval art shunned by Burrell, apart from minor purchases in 1925 and 1930. Similarly the fine collection of stained glass formed by the deeply religious Raymond Pitcairn (1885–1966) of Bryn Athyn, Pennsylvania, complemented rather than clashed with Burrell's, as it is confined fairly rigidly to the twelfth and thirteenth centuries whereas the latter's is concentrated in the Late Gothic period. One American collector who, like Burrell, continued to amass during and after the Depression was J. Paul Getty. He observed that in this period through financial pressures 'many of the strong hands that formerly held some of the finest examples of art on the face of the earth were forced to relax their grip'.

Burrell, with his innate antipathy to spending more money than was absolutely necessary, disliked any competition and could react strongly against it. Lord Eccles when a young man decided to try and buy a medieval tapestry at Sotheby's. He could only afford to bid up to £500 and the tapestry was knocked down to Burrell. After the sale he approached Eccles in considerable annoyance at being forced to go so high, saying:

Young man, you should not bid against me.

In May 1944, after the acquisition at Sotheby's of stained glass from the Eumorfopoulos Collection, Burrell wrote to Wilfred Drake expressing his pleasure that Philip Nelson had not attended the sale; before the auction he had been worried at the possibility of competition from this quarter which would undoubtedly have raised the price.

For the same reason he was very circumspect in his approach to a potential acquisition. He liked to 'circle round it' as he put it, in order to avoid raising the price by alerting the dealer to his keen interest. On occasions he went to extraordinary lengths to conceal his intentions in the saleroom from rivals. According to family tradition he once obtained a private preview of a sale by entering through a side entrance before the main doors of the auction house were opened. One of his saleroom stratagems was to get individuals unknown to the trade to bid for him. At auctions in which he was interested in several items he would not put all his eggs in one basket, but would commission various people to bid for different lots. To give but one example, at the sale in October 1938 of the contents of Formakin, Holms' house, Burrell obtained items through R. Morrison, Kirkhope and Son and Muirhead Moffat and Co. Burrell liked to attend sales in person, even if he was not bidding himself (sometimes he did) but had commissioned others to act for him. With John and Gertrude Hunt, of whom more will be said shortly, he evolved a strategy whereby they were to keep bidding on his behalf until he raised the bowler hat which he customarily wore. So carefully planned in advance were his bids that he never had cause to do so. This planning and self-discipline may be contrasted with Hearst's uncontrollable behaviour in the saleroom. His desire to possess was so great that he would forget all prior arrangements with his agents. Often the latter would bid up to the agreed price and then Hearst, terrified at the prospect of losing, would begin bidding for himself.

On occasions Burrell was outbid over some very worthwhile items because he was not prepared to go high enough. In 1925 he commissioned the Paris dealer Etienne Bignou to bid for two paintings by Chardin at the Michel Levy Collection Sale and for a Cézanne watercolour from the Gangnat Collection, but in all three cases he was unsuccessful; he just missed one of the Chardins, for it fetched 103,000 francs and Bignou was the under-bidder at 102,500. In July he did buy a picture then attributed to Chardin entitled *Pierrot Voleur* at the George Donaldson Sale at Hove. Three years later he failed in his attempts to buy the stained glass from the chapel windows of Ashridge House near Berkhamsted in Hertfordshire, and at the Sir Hercules Read Sale, a small German fifteenth-century tapestry altar frontal depicting the Holy Trinity. The latter was sold for £4,200 and Burrell may have based his bid on the £98 which it fetched thirty years earlier. His bid was nowhere near the actual price, as he told Wilfred Drake. He was eventually to acquire the tapestry in 1946 at the sale of Sir Humphrey Noble's collection. The Ashridge glass fetched £27,000, a large sum at the time and one that appalled Burrell: 'I think it is a wonderful price & much beyond its real value.' Bernard Rackham, Keeper of the Department of Ceramics at the Victoria and Albert Museum, did not share Burrell's views for he acquired it for the Museum. One can only concur with Rackham's judgement, for the Ashridge glass includes some very important sixteenth-century Cologne School panels from the Cistercian abbey of Mariawald and the Premonstratensian monastery at Steinfeld. It is precisely the type of glazing which appealed to Burrell and it would have graced his collection.

By the same token he also worried that he may have paid too much. In September 1938, in telling Drake that the consignment of English glass (mainly armorial) from the Hearst Collection had arrived, Burrell lamented that the prices were too high. He returned to the same theme in March of the following year:

> I have paid very full prices (in the times through which we are passing). I have to realise stock and get only *half* of what it cost so it is *very dear* glass. Please explain this to Roy Grosvenor Thomas.

(Grosvenor Thomas negotiated with Parish-Watson & Co. of New York for the Hearst glass.) Burrell should not have worried: his stained glass acquisitions from Randolph Hearst raised this part of his collection to one of international importance, fit to stand comparison with the holdings of the Victoria and Albert Museum and the Cloisters.

Burrell was equally reluctant to spend other people's money when he was in a position to influence the decision. Nothing has come to light about his activities as a Trustee of both the National Galleries of Scotland and the National Gallery of British Art, apart from one revealing anecdote. In 1936 the firm of Wildenstein & Co. offered Edinburgh a masterpiece by Gauguin, *Three Tahitians*. Burrell was present at the Board meeting in April when the purchase was considered and was instrumental in the decision to turn it down on the grounds that it was too expensive. His reaction can hardly be put down to any prejudice on his part against the artist, for in June of the same year he bought a chalk study of a Breton girl by him (this was a preliminary sketch for the painting *Four Breton Women Talking* now in Munich). As he paid a mere £150 it was probably only the price-tag on the *Three Tahitians* which put him off. It may indeed have convinced him of the desirability of owning a Gauguin himself. Fortunately the matter ended happily, for another member of the Board, the painter Sir D.Y.

Gauguin's THREE TAHITIANS: Burrell was opposed to its acquisition by the National Galleries of Scotland because he felt it was too expensive. It was given to the National Galleries 24 years later. (National Galleries of Scotland)

One of the few acquisitions for which Burrell's efforts to reduce the price were unsuccessful: the Jacobite linen cloth, traditionally believed to have been used as Bonnie Prince Charlie's christening apron. The vendor, Muirhead Moffat, refused to budge from his asking price, and won!

Cameron, persuaded his friend Sir Alexander Maitland to buy the picture and in 1960 he gave it to the National Galleries in Edinburgh.

Between the wars Burrell avoided the large-scale purchases from long-formed and well-known collections which had made J. Pierpont Morgan's acquisitions so easy, not to say expensive. The exceptions are selected aspects of Hearst's collection (from 1938) and those collections formed by fellow-Scots which he knew well: Burrell was a buyer in some quantities at the 1927 and 1935 sales of the pictures belonging to the Coats family and of the remains of Leonard Gow's splendid holdings of Chinese ceramics. On the whole, like Henry Walters, he preferred to buy works of art either singly or in small amounts from a wide variety of sources. Virtually everything came through dealers, either directly or through their bidding on his behalf at auctions. Wherever Burrell went he frequented their premises, whether in Chester, Brighton, Bournemouth, Glasgow, Edinburgh or better-known art centres. Although he occasionally patronised dealers like Julius Böhler in Munich, his main hunting grounds were London and Paris.

Randolph Hearst complained that, 'When I try to buy anything, the price has a habit of going up and up.' When Burrell went after something he did his utmost to ensure that the price went down and down. Like the American store magnate Samuel Kress, he got as much pleasure out of haggling as he did from ownership. The Purchase Books contain a number of references to 'special price' or 'special discount', as in 1919 when he bought some antique lace from a Brighton dealer for £136 less a 'special discount' of £21. Burrell did not always come out on top in the bargaining. In 1933 Muirhead Moffat sold him a linen cloth embroidered with the arms of thirteen Jacobite families and purportedly used as Bonnie Prince Charlie's christening apron.

> We had it for some years. Sir William knew this and phoned me. We wanted £175 for it.
> 'It's too dear,' he said. 'I'll give you £140.'
> I refused. Then he came to £150 and then £160.
> 'A Jacobite glass can be worth £500,' I reminded him. 'And the apron is surely worth as much.'
> But neither of us would budge, and the deal was off. However, a few days later his cheque for £175 came in.

With dealers he was approaching for the first time he would even conceal his identity for fear that if they knew who he was the price would be inflated. A London dealer named Hans Calmann recalled his first encounter with Burrell in 1938. The old man shuffled into his shop one day and purchased, after much bargaining, a first century AD Han dynasty earthenware watch-dog and a vase. Only after the transaction

Han dynasty earthenware watch-dog purchased from Hans Calmann in 1938 after much haggling.

—127—

was concluded did Burrell introduce himself. Calmann was very impressed by Burrell and considered that unlike many other wealthy collectors he had good judgement and knew what he wanted.

Burrell made much less of an impact initially with Jacques Seligmann and his son Germain, as the latter has recorded:

> One of the most interesting of our English [sic] clients was Sir William Burrell, the Scottish shipping magnate to whom I made one of my earliest personal sales. My father was still alive [Jacques Seligmann died in 1923] and we were together at Sagan when Mr William Burrell (not yet knighted) was announced; the name meant nothing to either of us. It was my father's custom to meet everyone who came, though he might afterwards leave me or someone else in charge. On this occasion we both went out to greet the visitor. After the usual amenities, the three of us went together through the different Gothic and Renaissance rooms, the periods in which Burrell had expressed an interest. There my father left us, not that he had something of immediate import to do, but he had not been impressed by Burrell's comments and thought he was wasting his time. Burrell did not strike me as having a collector's potentialities, financially or in taste. At that time he was perhaps fifty years of age, of the lean wiry type that changes little in appearance in the middle years, and he spoke with a Scotch burr so marked that at times I had considerable difficulty understanding him.
>
> I was left to cope with the rest of the visit as well as I could. We had been walking about for more than two hours . . . and I was at my wit's end. Nothing seemed to retain his attention and he asked for few prices. On the other hand, I reasoned that since this man had already stayed this long, it must be proof of his desire to purchase something. Finally, in desperation, I took him to one of the lateral wings of Sagan where there were stored, without much order, a lot of items of lesser interest, left-overs, so to speak, from a collection which my father had bought several years before solely for the sake of acquiring three Gothic sculptures of great beauty. It was an inspiration, for at last he found there two Flemish wood sculptures, angels of strictly decorative character, which took his fancy. Now I thought the matter would be quickly settled, but I was quite mistaken. With true Scotch canniness, he bargained, and another half-hour went by before the deal was closed. Happily, the objects were of little importance and he could get them almost at his own price.

The first recorded purchase by Burrell from Jacques Seligmann is in May 1922, and is not of two Flemish angels but of a Flemish wood figure of St Christopher. His meeting could, however, have taken place earlier, at any time from 1909, when Seligmann purchased the Hôtel de Sagan as his Paris premises. It is likely that Burrell was merely testing the water, using the opportunity to assess his man rather than make a significant purchase. It was a tactic he adopted with other dealers. Tom Honeyman recounted a similar tale about his first meeting with Burrell in 1929, when he was working for Alex Reid and Lefevre at their Glasgow premises:

> . . . Sir William put me through my paces in what must have been the forerunner of BBC quiz programmes. He also gave me some illuminating views on art and art dealing and, finally, after some bargaining, bought a Crawhall drawing. Throughout the afternoon I glowed with satisfaction – my first contact with the Burrell Collection. Two hours later I got a telegram from Edinburgh cancelling the purchase of the Crawhall – he had plenty of them – and ending with 'good wishes'.

When Germain Seligmann and Honeyman knew him better they both came to like and respect him. And this was the common reaction amongst dealers with whom he had the longest associations, even though he was not an easy man with whom to do business. In addition to his love of bargaining he would go to remarkable lengths to assure himself of the authenticity of an object. Muirhead Moffat recalled that Burrell's first questions, before even looking at a possible acquisition, were, 'Is it dead right? Any restorations?' Even those members of the trade whom he had known for years would find him seeking a second opinion and if it was adverse and he had already bought the object, returning it and demanding his money back or a credit against future acquisitions. In 1938, for example, he cancelled the purchase for £550 of an oak pulpit from the Hearst Collection: 'Rejected as too much made up. Vetted by Mr. Hunt and Mr. Partridge.' He was equally exacting when it came to determining the degree of restoration prospective purchases had undergone. The Purchase Books contain a number of descriptions which include comments such as 'Guaranteed with original polychrome' for sculpture, or 'Guaranteed not repaired' in the case of a tapestry or carpet. The entry for the large tapestry depicting *The Anniversary of Hector's Funeral*, purchased in 1936 from Arnold Seligmann, even went so far as to state that: 'This Tapestry does not show more than 5% (five per cent) repair not counting the inscription', although how anyone could be quite so specific is a matter for conjecture. Gertrude Hunt remembers how Burrell had her husband crawling over tapestries and carpets to get a precise estimate of the amount of re-weaving.

A large number of dealers occur in the Purchase Books for the inter-war years, including David Croal Thomson (pictures), Balian (Near Eastern carpets) and Owen Evan Thomas (treen – Thomas was the author of a standard book on the subject). The earlier Chinese ceramics and bronzes tended to come from T.J. Larkin and Bluett and the late Ming and Kangxi wares from S.M. Franck & Co. and H.R. Hancock. Amongst the Parisian dealers patronised by Burrell the most important were Maurice Stora and the firms founded by the brothers and bitter rivals Arnold and Jacques Seligmann. Through these three

Portrait of the art dealer David Croal Thomson, painted by P.W. Steer in 1895. Burrell purchased a number of important pictures from him, including works by Degas and Daumier. (Tate Gallery)

Burrell obtained some of his best tapestries; he also purchased some fine paintings from Georges Bernheim and Allard.

One name conspicuous by its absence from this list is the flamboyant Joseph Duveen, the most remarkable of all art dealers. He does figure briefly in the Purchase Book for 1917. On 29 October and 28 November Burrell purchased from him a Stuart arm-chair, a Hispano–Moresque dish and a Chinese blue vase at a total cost of £200. Thereafter there are no recorded transactions between Duveen and Burrell. The tale goes that Burrell tried to sell back an item he had purchased from him in part-exchange for something else. Duveen refused and Burrell, as we have already seen, not one to forget a slight, never did business with him again. In the period of Burrell's Trusteeship of the National Gallery of British Art, to which Duveen had been a generous benefactor (as well he might, considering how many paintings by the British eighteenth-century masters crossed the Atlantic through his agency) an angry exchange took place between the two men at a reception there. A clash between strong characters of such differing temperaments was sooner or later bound to occur. Duveen, who viewed Hearst as small fry because he only spent approximately five million dollars in his galleries, could never have treated Burrell as a client worthy of serious consideration and must have disliked his practice of haggling. The frugal and unassuming Scotsman for his part must have abhorred Duveen's ostentatious behaviour and, more to the point, his enormous prices. Burrell was not the only important collector to steer clear of Duveen – Henry Walters was another and for similar reasons.

In addition to the names mentioned above there was a select inner group, the members of which were as close to Burrell as any individuals outside his immediate family. They comprised Alex Reid (until his death in 1928), Frank Surgey, Wilfred Drake, Frank Partridge, Peter Sparks, and John Hunt and his wife Gertrude. With them Burrell rarely if ever resorted to haggling. It was hardly a tightly-knit group, for Burrell was very careful to give the impression to each of them that he was his sole trusted adviser. In conversation with the survivors and those who knew them well it is striking how unaware they were of how much Burrell was also buying from their rivals.

Some account of Drake and Surgey has been given in connection with Hutton Castle, and also of Alex Reid in Chapter Two. After his death the connection was maintained by his son A.J. McNeill Reid, who went into partnership with the Lefevre Galleries in London. Frank Partridge (d.1952) was the son of a Hertfordshire shoe-maker and as a boy had been apprenticed to a draper. This was not to his liking and before long he joined his brother's antique business; towards the end of the last century he established his own firm in premises in King Street, stocking it with everything he owned. Within a few days of opening he had the good fortune to attract the attention of the soap magnate William Hesketh Lever (later Lord Leverhulme) and within a short while his courage and boldness carried him to the forefront of art dealers, aided by that essential ingredient, good fortune, instanced by his surviving the sinking in 1915 of the 'Lusitania'. In addition to Burrell and Lord Leverhulme other distinguished clients were Queen Mary and John D. Rockefeller. At that time Partridge specialised in oak furniture and *objets d'art* of the sixteenth and seventeenth centuries, including needlework, and Chinese ceramics – the emphasis today has *See plate 17* switched towards English and French furniture of the eighteenth century.

Burrell's first visit was an occasion which has become part of Partridge family lore. There appeared in the premises at 12.30 one Saturday a middle-aged man who without identifying himself announced:

'I'm just a Scotsman down for the day and I would like to look around.' After an hour's perusal he wrote down the five items of furniture and needlework he wanted which turned out to be the best things there. Burrell's first recorded purchase from Partridge is in February 1916 when he bought three eighteenth-century pieces of needlework, so it seems likely that this first meeting occurred before the Purchase Books began in 1911. This was the beginning of a long association between Burrell and Frank Partridge. More works of art came from this source either directly or through Partridge's agency than from any other single art dealer.

In some ways the most interesting member of the inner sanctum is John Hunt. Certainly he can be the only art dealer to have earned the joint but distinct accolades of an academic *Festschrift* and an obituary by a cleric. His tall and slender figure was well known to the curators of all the leading museums with important collections of medieval European art and his judgement and knowledge were highly respected. One reason for this high reputation was his love of and sympathy for medieval art, which sometimes clashed with his commercial interests; unlike many dealers he collected for himself in the very field in which he traded. I retain a vivid impression of John Hunt showing me almost with awe a pomander which he had just bought; the reverence stemmed from his belief that it had belonged to a French king and he could scarcely believe that it had come to rest in his hands.

Although his father had collected and he himself had been interested in ancient artefacts while still at school, Hunt entered the art world through personal misfortune. His chosen career was medicine, but while still a student had to give it up for health reasons. He then joined a firm of antique furniture dealers and when Burrell first met him in 1932 he was working as a buyer for Acton Surgey. Burrell quickly formed a high opinion of his abilities and when the firm gave Hunt notice and was unwilling to give Burrell his address he went to the trouble of tracking him down. The first recorded purchase from Hunt is in November 1933 and from then onwards until the outbreak of the war he became Burrell's trusted adviser on medieval objects, although Burrell also had the occasional Oriental rug or piece of Chinese or Near Eastern pottery from him. Burrell was already an important collector of medieval tapestries, furniture and stained glass before he became acquainted with Hunt, but his purchases of the smaller *objets d'art* of this period, particularly Limoges enamels, ivories and bronzes, only attained any significance through Hunt's agency.

Burrell made a similar arrangement with Hunt to that which he had with Frank Surgey, Drake and Frank Partridge, namely that he would pay a commission, usually of 5% or 10%, on everything he had from him or on which he advised or bid on his behalf at auction. This suited both parties. From Burrell's point of view it kept the price down, at least in the saleroom, for Hunt and the others would not buy for themselves and charge him a grossly marked-up figure. On the other hand it gave the dealers a more-or-less guaranteed income in uncertain times. Muirhead Moffat negotiated a variant to this formula whereby if something came up at auction which he wanted for his shop, he would say his price was £100, or whatever it was, and the commission would be half of what Burrell saved. This seemingly more lucrative arrangement from Moffat's point of view in the event seems to have back-fired on him, for Burrell never liked it and it almost certainly explains why he bought only rarely through this source. It is also worth remembering that Burrell's sagacity and dislike of paying high prices (and the care with which he scrutinised sale catalogues) were formidable obstacles in the path of anyone who thought of walking the path of independence. In addition Burrell made a special concession to Hunt's own love of medieval art and agreed that the latter did not have to offer everything to him, but could collect for himself. It is interesting to note that the Hunt Collection now displayed in the National Institute for Higher Education in Limerick contains several items which have companions in the Burrell Collection. In at least one instance a conflict arose over

The English ivory 'brown Madonna' which the Hunts refused to sell to Burrell (The Cloisters, New York); and (right) the boxwood VIRGIN AND CHILD they obtained for him as a substitute. Both are of 14th-century date.

this concession. In 1932 John Hunt's German-born wife Gertrude gave him as a birthday present a superb English fourteenth-century ivory group of the Virgin and Child, known from its colouring as the 'brown Madonna'. Burrell wanted this very badly and tried to persuade the Hunts to part with it. As they refused to do so Burrell told Hunt to find something similar. Eventually he came up with the boxwood Virgin and Child which was carved in Eastern France during the early fourteenth century. It cost Burrell the large sum (for him) of £500, a price that reflected its high quality. Fortunately such awkward situations did not arise very often, largely because the Hunts preferred the early medieval period, whereas Burrell's tastes were much more for Late Gothic. Burrell occasionally revealed to the Hunts a generous, considerate side to his nature. He once gave back to Mrs Hunt a tiny Mesopotamian amulet which she had sold him because she liked it so much and wanted to wear it.

There were also lighter moments which showed that even as he moved into old age Burrell did not lose that dry, rather pawky sense of humour he had displayed in his younger years. Not long before the Second World War began a minor collector named King entered Hunt's shop in Bury Street and saw him showing an object to a rather fragile old man. The latter spoke with a strong Scottish accent which prompted the following dialogue:

King: 'You are Scottish, Sir?'
Aged Gentleman: 'Aye.'
King: 'Do you know Sir William Burrell?'
Aged Gentleman: 'Aye, and I'm what's left of him!'

Burrell could also still tell a story against himself. In 1925 he had given Kelvingrove Art Gallery a group of paintings with the stipulation that they had to be displayed together. One day he went to have a look at them and asked the attendant in the room in which they were hung about them. Burrell told Tom Honeyman that the man, who did not recognise him, had replied: 'Oh! I don't know much about them. We've got to keep them together, that's the condition, but we'll likely scatter them when the old buffer dies.' His words were very nearly prophetic, because this is precisely what some of the officials of Glasgow Corporation would have liked to have done with the entire Collection.

The Hunts and the other members of Burrell's inner group of agents and advisers respected his age and memory, but there were differing opinions among them about his knowledge. Peter Sparks did not think that he knew very much about Chinese art and maintained that he dissuaded him from buying more things than he actually acquired. Burrell himself would not have disputed that his academic knowledge even in his favourite medieval field was deficient. For instance, in his correspondence with Drake over the Devon churches tour he requested an explanation of the Seven Sacraments ('don't know all 7 Sacraments'). This was a general iconographical query, but he had to ask similar questions about objects in his collection. In 1929 Drake received a letter from him wanting to know what the stained-glass quarries represented which he had bought the previous year at the Hercules Read Sale. The letter ends: '. . . I like to understand what I have if I can.'

Burrell's delight on discovering, through his interpretation of the researches of a member of the despised academic breed, Dr S.H. Steinberg, of a tenuous historical connection between Hutton Castle and his stained-glass panel depicting Beatrix van Valkenburg was almost childlike. He wrote with enthusiasm to Drake: *See plate 18*

> The position is even more interesting than before. Edward I slept in Hutton Castle in 1296 the night before he attacked and took Berwick-on-Tweed. He slept in the Tower bedroom and as it was the only bedroom in the 'Keep' you may be sure that his cousin Richard Plantagenet – Beatrix de Falkenburgh's stepson – slept in the same room so that the position is much closer even than the fact that Richard was killed at the siege of Berwick. Her little panel is today only a few feet away from the bedroom in which her stepson no doubt slept.

Notwithstanding Burrell's interest in the historical associations and iconography of his pieces it was subordinate to their intrinsic value and aesthetic appeal. He was keenly aware of both factors and his visual perception and amazing memory caused dealers to be very careful. Shortly before the correspondence regarding the Devon tour, Drake wrote to Parish-Watson about the sale of two German thirteenth-century stained glass panels belonging to Hearst:

> I had to point out to Sir W.B. that the ww [window] was 'Composite' as H's book [Gottfried Heinesdorff, *Die Glasmalerei. Ihre Technik und Ihre Geschichte* (Berlin, 1914), in which the panels are shown before additions were made] is well known over here (Sir W. has a copy himself at H.C.).

He suggested in another letter that the price should be reduced by a quarter.

Burrell had his likes and dislikes, even within the medieval period. The Hunts had the greatest difficulty in persuading him to buy twelfth-century objects. In 1936, for instance, they prevailed upon him to buy the superb English or German bronze known as the *Temple Pyx* *See plate 19* from the Pitt-Rivers Collection only by appealing to his patriotism: if he didn't aquire it it would certainly be snapped up by an American museum or private collector. Even the Hunts were not always successful. The year after the acquisition of the *Temple Pyx* Burrell cancelled the purchase of a marble figure of an apostle or prophet from Le Pons near Montpelier. The price of £1,050 may have been an important factor in this decision, but so surely were his aesthetic prejudices.

On the whole Burrell's dealers served him well in the inter-war years. Some pieces, particularly furniture, had been restored more than Burrell was led to believe, but the number of fakes purchased in this period is small. The purchases of spurious medieval objects tend to be confined to the early 1920's, indicating that Burrell gradually learned to be more discriminating. It is doubtful in the vast majority of cases if the dealers knowingly sold him forgeries, if only for fear of killing the golden goose. A rare instance when one suspects otherwise is that of an enamel plaque purporting to be of late twelfth-century date. The vendor's description in the Purchase Book is to say the least disingenuous: '. . . very fine in drawing and so rare in type that one could never find another like it.' Exactly.

To recognise most of the fakes for what they are would have demanded photographic records and a degree of expertise scarcely available at the time. For example, it would have taken a true specialist to recognise that the two copper-gilt figures purchased in Paris as '14th Cent. French' in 1922 were copied from the shrine of St Gertrude at Nivelles in Belgium (the shrine was almost totally destroyed in 1940), or that the oak figure of St Margaret bought in 1927 was an excellent modern reproduction of the original in the Gruuthuse Museum,

Burrell burns his fingers: two copper-gilt figures copied, probably in the late 19th century, from the shrine of St Gertrude of Nivelles in Belgium. Burrell bought them in 1922 as 14th-century French originals.

Bruges. Several forgeries or modern copies (the two are not necessarily synonymous) have only been revealed very recently. An alabaster relief of a mourner from a tomb formerly in the Philip Nelson Collection which Burrell purchased in the same year as the St Margaret remained unsuspected until 1975, when it was identified in the *Scottish Art Review* as a copy of a tomb relief in the Walters Art Gallery, Baltimore. The process of evaluation is a constant one, and no doubt other fakes or heavily restored items will be revealed by future researchers, but with some degree of confidence it can be stated that taking into account just how wide Burrell spread himself in his collecting he burned his fingers surprisingly rarely.

Re-evaluation also has a credit side and there are several pieces which in recent years have been shown to be of greater importance than either Burrell or the dealers were aware. None more so than a stained-glass panel depicting the prophet Jeremiah. This was purchased in 1923 from Arnold Seligmann as 'a bearded saint holding a scroll' for £114 5s 10d, a sum bearing no relation to its value since its identification as one of the earliest surviving examples of European glass, commissioned around 1140–5 by Abbot Suger for the abbey of St Denis just outside Paris. On a more modest level, a pair of polychromed wooden angels playing musical instruments obtained in 1931 have recently been revealed as the work of one of the leading Tyrolean Late Gothic sculptors, Hans Klocker of Bozen.

See plate 20

A detailed examination of the Purchase Books between 1917 and the early 1940's reveals the difference between Burrell the collector before the fleet sales and Burrell the collector after the fleet sales. The scale and range of his acquisitions in these years is by any standards astonishing. The purchase of nearly four thousand items is recorded, excluding the modern furnishings for Hutton Castle and jewellery. Moreover there are a number of pieces known to have been added to his collection between these years which are not mentioned in the Purchase Books. Between 1918 and 1920 Burrell made some major additions to his stained glass from the Costessey Hall Collection, including the early sixteenth-century St John the Evangelist windows and Tree of Jesse panels from Rouen which were referred to in the previous chapter. Also not recorded in the Purchase Books is a William Maris painting of a dead pigeon, acquired in the late 1920's from the artist and writer Eliot Hodgkin. He was very fond of it but was forced to offer it to Burrell in order to pay the rent:

> [Burrell] asked me what I wanted for it. I told him £17 10s. my quarter's rent. He agreed & took the picture without argument, telling me to be at the station the next morning when he would be leaving for Glasgow, when he would give me the cash. Night of anxiety, but he was there all right & gave me the money!

Burrell added to most areas of the Collection simultaneously, with the exception of the Ancient Civilisations, less than half a dozen objects of which were acquired in the inter-war years. Near Eastern pottery and metalwork purchases were also almost non-existent. Until the late 1920's very little stained glass is recorded in the Purchase Books. With these exceptions, every other major section of the Collection was increased by fresh additions almost every year, be it Chinese ceramics, Oriental carpets, medieval tapestries, furniture, pictures or silver. The record of his activities in Paris during July and August 1933 indicates his catholic tastes. In this period he purchased from six dealers two Degas pastels, a fifteenth-century stone bust of the Virgin and no fewer than nine tapestries, including the German altar frontal depicting the Adoration of the Magi with the family of the donor Erasmus Schurstab, and a fragment from the famous late fourteenth-century Apocalypse series at Angers.

The majority of purchases comprised English furniture, table glass and silver of the late seventeenth and early eighteenth centuries. Burrell's furniture buying was at its peak in 1925 and 1926, when ninety and eighty items respectively were acquired with a view to completing the furnishings of Hutton Castle. English late sixteenth-early eighteenth-century needlework and Chinese ceramics were obtained in considerable numbers. The Chinese ceramics were overwhelmingly of the Kangxi period and in particular *famille verte* and other multi-coloured wares, but included a sprinkling of earlier pieces, most of which were Ming, with a few Song and Tang items; some of the most important of these joined the Collection in 1943. The acquisition of Chinese bronzes was at a smaller and more sporadic rate than it had been between the years 1911 and 1916. The majority were of the Shang, Han or Ming dynasties.

Although Burrell was spreading his net very wide, at times he tended to concentrate on particular fields. Between 1917 and 1928 pictures seem to have been his prime interest. To his continuing taste for the Hague and Barbizon School artists and the Glasgow Boys, in these years was added a full-scale appreciation of Degas and, to a lesser degree, of Manet. He also flirted briefly with *plein-air* Impressionism and in 1920 and 1923 he purchased three minor works by Pissarro and Sisley's *The Bell-Tower, Noisy-le-Roi: Autumn*. Almost certainly Alex Reid pushed him in this direction, although he never persuaded him to embrace Impressionism wholeheartedly. With this in mind it is remarkable that Burrell ventured even further afield. We have already seen that in 1925 he made an unsuccessful attempt to purchase a Cézanne. It was more than a decade later before a work by this artist did enter his collection and it was a masterpiece: *Le Château de Médan*. It was bought from A.J. McNeill Reid and in common with several other

23 Three expensive purchases: the DIETRICHSTEIN CARPET bought in 1939 for £3,000; the BURY CHEST, which cost £2,500 in 1941; and a set of three Jacobean silver-gilt steeple cups. The last was one of a number of major acquisitions from William Randolph Hearst's collection which Burrell made in the late 1930's and early 1940's, and in 1952–54. The carpet and the steeple cups (for which he paid £3,900) are his most expensive single purchases in these sections of the Collection.

24 Monticelli's THE BAZAAR, MARSEILLES: Burrell considered his re-purchase of this picture in 1942 as his first stroke of luck in many years.

25 Two fields to which Burrell gave priority after the Second World War were Chinese ceramics and jades. Here is a Ming porcelain ewer of c. 1600; and a double cylindrical jade vase of the 13th–15th centuries AD.

26 *Burrell's most expensive acquisition ever:* PORTRAIT OF A GENTLEMAN, *attributed to Frans Hals, for which he paid £14,500 in 1948.*

*27 Second time lucky! The German
tapestry altar frontal of the early
fifteenth century for which Burrell
bid unsuccessfully in 1928. It finally
entered the Collection in 1946.*

French pictures in Burrell's collection it had an interesting history. It depicts Zola's house and was for a time in the possession of Gauguin, who described it in glowing terms in one of his letters. Gauguin himself was an artist never really appreciated by McNeill Reid's father and it is significant that he is only represented in the Collection by the chalk study of a Breton girl, and this was purchased eight years after Alex Reid's death in 1928.

By the time the Cézanne and Gauguin were purchased Burrell was concentrating on Late Gothic tapestries rather than pictures. In 1933, for example, he bought sixteen tapestries compared with only six pictures, and in 1935 the respective totals were 35 and eleven. On the whole his tapestries cost him more than his paintings: in 1937 the price of the late fifteenth-century tapestry with scenes of Courtship and Marriage was much more than the Cézanne (£6,390 compared with £3,500). The price of several tapestries exceeded the £8,000 he paid in

A rare venture towards the avant-gard: Cézanne's LE CHÂTEAU DE MÉDAN, purchased by Burrell in 1937.

See plate 21

See plate 22

1926 for his most expensive picture, Daumier's *Le Meunier, son Fils et l'Ane*. Five tapestries were purchased for £10,000 or more.

Burrell's acquisitions in other fields seldom cost him anything like these amounts. In Chinese art his most expensive bronzes were two Shang and Han vessels, both of which cost him £500. Chinese ceramics were much cheaper, with the exception of a pair of Ming vases purchased in 1925 for £1,650 and a pair of Kangxi tapered black vases for which he paid the very large sum of £7,750 in 1934 and 1935. The most costly pieces of furniture were an extremely rare inlaid table dated 1567, which came from Partridge's in 1924 for £2,750, and an Elizabethan oak banqueting table bought for £3,000 two years later. Oak was always Burrell's favourite wood. 'Take it from me,' he told Leslie Dawson of Partridge's, 'you start with oak and then go to mahogany and other woods. But mark my words, you always come back to oak.'

In the late 1930's and early 1940's Burrell was occasionally prepared to spend much larger sums than before on works of art other than tapestries or pictures, chiefly because some splendid pieces came on to the market and could be obtained at what were bargain prices. In 1939 he paid the Royal Bank of Scotland £2,750 for a famous seventeenth-century Persian carpet, known after a previous owner as the Wagner Garden Carpet; it later belonged to John A. Holms and Lorimer had designed a special room for it at Formakin. In the following year the

See plate 23

purchase of the Persian carpet known as the Dietrichstein carpet cost Burrell £3,000; at the time it was believed to date from the second half of the seventeenth century and to have been given by the Shah of Persia to the Empress Maria Theresa, but it is now considered to have been woven in the nineteenth century. In 1941 he acquired from Colonel Colville for £2,500 the fourteenth-century oak coffer with a painted lid known as the *Bury Chest*.

Some of Burrell's most expensive purchases in these years were from Randolph Hearst's Collection and included some very tasty crumbs from this rich man's table. Although for the stained glass he paid out much larger sums than ever before (and grumbled accordingly) his acquisitions in this field were outstanding and worth even then many times what he paid for them. The large three-light window painted in *c*.1440 for the former Carmelite church at Boppard on the Rhine cost £1,600, a French fifteenth-century window of two lights was purchased for £1,800 and a series of twelve panels from North Germany for £1,760.

See plate 23

Burrell did not just buy stained glass from Hearst: the most expensive acquisition of all was a magnificent set of Jacobean silver-gilt steeple cups, which cost £3,900. Purchases from the Hearst Collection did not stop in 1939 and after the war some even more remarkable bargains were obtained.

Although the format of the Purchase Book entries remained unchanged from that established in 1911, the amount of information given increased markedly in the inter-war years. Burrell ceased to make sketches of the objects, but dimensions are invariably recorded and the descriptions are much more detailed. The entry in the 1934 Purchase Book for the *Boar Hunt* tapestry includes a description in French transcribed from the notes of the previous owner, and sometimes dealers' letters are quoted. Extracts from three letters from Frank Partridge concerning the pair of Kangxi black vases mentioned above are given in the 1935 Purchase Books:

> 'They are the most outstanding pair of square blacks in the world.' 26 September 1935.
> 'Yes, I certainly mean I consider the pair of Square Blacks to be second to none in existence.' 24 September 1935.
> 'You are now the proud possessor as I have told you before of the square vases of unsurpassed quality and perfection.' 3 October 1935.

Information on the provenance is occasionally given and so is an explanation of the iconography. Burrell was also aware of the importance of including bibliographical references. In a few instances his obsession with obtaining objects at less than their current market values shows through, as in the case of a Jacobean silver-mounted crystal jug acquired in 1941 for £297. At the end of the description is a note on a similar item sold at Christie's in 1924 to Hearst for £6,000: 'and he sold it *c.*1939 to I think Lord Bute for abt £2000'. Some of the descriptions are very long, extending to three or four pages in the Purchase Books. There are just two notes unrelated to his collection and more at home in a personal journal. At the beginning of the 1934 Book is a note that he and his wife were in Jamaica from January to April, and the outbreak of war is recorded in the Purchase Book for 1939. With these exceptions the Books are devoid of personal comment.

The Books also show that Burrell was not buying solely with the invested proceeds of his ship-owning but continued his pre-First World War policy of selling and exchanging works of art, albeit on a reduced scale. His motives for disposing of a particular work of art are in almost every case a matter of speculation. The only exception is the two Peploe pictures sold in 1942 and 1943: in 1936 Burrell told Honeyman, 'I think I have too many of him and may sell one or two.' Probably he got tired of some things or was offered an attractive deal if he was prepared to make an exchange. The largest category of items traded in or sold was seventeenth and eighteenth-century furniture and most of the transactions involved Partridge's. Some of the exchanges were quite substantial, as in 1934 when an acquisition from Frank Partridge of Chinese porcelain and an Elizabethan oak buffet for £6,752 was offset by the return of three oak buffets, a suite of Chippendale furniture, a set of six

The silver-mounted crystal jug purchased in 1941; Burrell compared it with one bought by Hearst in 1924 for £6,000.

Chippendale chairs, two settees and ten needlework chair seats for a total of £4,410, leaving Burrell to pay only £2,342. Not just minor items passed out of Burrell's possession in this way, but also some substantial pieces. Some of the departures are much to be regretted, including a Late Gothic tapestry depicting a hawking scene for which Burrell in 1927 received a credit of £11,010, and a set of five English alabasters forming an altarpiece returned to the vendor in the following year for £1,000. In 1937 Burrell even parted with the pair of Kangxi black vases which he had only recently acquired; he at least showed a profit on the transaction, receiving £8,000 for them. More serious was the loss of several important pictures, including two Manet pastels, one being a portrait of Marie Laurent, sold to Reid and Lefevre in 1937 and 1943 for a total of £4,600, a Millet sold for £1,500 and several works by Daumier.

Between the two World Wars Burrell purchased at such a rate that soon there was no longer sufficient space in the living rooms and even the servants' quarters at Hutton to house his acquisitions, which by 1944 totalled approximately 6,000 items. They were stored in crates in the garages and outhouses. The sales and exchanges and the gift in 1925 of 27 oil paintings and 51 water-colours, pastels and drawings to Kelvingrove Art Gallery did not alleviate the storage problem to any marked extent, but it was solved temporarily by loans. On the outbreak of war in 1939 the National Galleries in Edinburgh, the Tate Gallery and more than thirty museums and cathedrals in England, Scotland and Wales had on loan substantial parts of Burrell's collection. This dispersal was not intended to be any more than short-term, for by then he had formed the intention not only of amassing a permanent collection, but of handing it over in its entirety to public ownership.

Precisely when he made up his mind to do this will probably never be established, but it seems that around 1930, when he was approaching seventy, he began to give the eventual fate of his collection very serious thought. In 1931 Burrell attended the annual dinner of the British Antiques Dealers Association, at which Frank Surgey, in proposing the toast to the guests, stated that it was a source of satisfaction to know that Burrell's collection would not leave the country. A decision to keep it within Great Britain must have been quite easy for a man of Burrell's patriotic views, but to find a suitable recipient who could meet his stringent conditions was another matter. From the outset he insisted that his collection must be in a smokeless zone in order to protect the tapestries and carpets from atmospheric pollution, and yet it should be near a large city so that it could be enjoyed by as many people as possible. Moreover the maintenance of the Collection had to be at the expense of the recipients; as this entailed large galleries to display the textiles the cost was going to be considerable. A converted private house comparable in scale with Sir John Soane's museum in Lincoln's Inn Fields in London or even Frick's residence in New York was out of the question. With trusted advisers like the Hunts and Frank Surgey, Burrell explored various possibilities. He also consulted Sir Kenneth Clark (later Lord Clark) and Sir Eric Maclagan, respectively Directors of the National Gallery and the Victoria and Albert Museum. Burrell's native city of Glasgow does not seem to have been an early candidate and London and its environs was for long seriously considered, with the support of Surgey and Clark. The former felt that such a rich collection deserved an international audience and when St John's Lodge, the former town house of the Marquises of Bute on the Inner Circle in Regent's Park became available, he strongly pressed its merits as a future home for the Collection. Similarly Clark suggested a house with grounds large enough to accommodate galleries for tapestries and carpets which he found in Hampstead, opposite Jack Straw's Castle. Clark also persuaded the London County Council to help finance the project but with war approaching nothing came of it. According to Honeyman, the LCC itself made various suggestions including a site on the South Bank near Waterloo Bridge; ironically this was almost certainly the space now occupied by the Hayward Gallery, where the Burrell Collection in 1975 received its first London showing, the success of which almost certainly played a large part in securing financial support from the Government for its eventual home.

It is doubtful if Burrell gave his blessing to any of these proposals, in spite of their comparatively rural settings in Regent's Park and Hampstead, for none of the sites was free from atmospheric pollution. In the event St John's Lodge in 1935 was leased by the fledgling Institute of Archaeology of London University, the brain-child of the flamboyant Sir Mortimer Wheeler. It is now used by the Directorate of the Royal Parks.

His advocacy of the capital city notwithstanding, Kenneth Clark also often said to Burrell that he should donate the Collection to Glasgow. Although Burrell must have given the suggestion serious consideration he had not made up his mind before the outbreak of war in 1939. As late as November of that year the manor house at East Barsham in Norfolk, built by Sir Henry Fermor in 1520–30, was put forward as a suitable home for the Collection. Apart from Haddon Hall in Derbyshire and Compton Wynyates in Warwickshire it is hard to think of a more appropriate setting for Burrell's tapestries, stained glass and fifteenth and sixteenth-century furniture and objects (albeit not the Oriental items) than this delightful brick mansion, described by Sir Nikolaus Pevsner as 'the picture-book ideal of an Early Tudor house'. Burrell rejected it unseen, on the grounds that it was too far from any

major city. According to Mrs Surgey, about this time he decided that the Collection would not go out of Scotland. Through his Trusteeship of the National Galleries he had enjoyed close connections with the cultural life of Edinburgh, but if the Scottish capital was ever a serious candidate the actions of its authorities in removing Burrell's iron railings at Hutton for scrap without adequate compensation removed it from the scene. This left Glasgow as the only possibility, yet even then he hesitated to commit himself. In October 1940 he consulted Honeyman about the disposal of several pictures including the gift of two to Kelvingrove. Moreover as late as March 1943 Burrell wrote to Wilfred Drake in characteristically cautious tone: 'I am going over all the photographs adding what information I can for the benefit of those who may get the things.'

One evening in December 1943, Tom Honeyman received a telephone call from Burrell summoning him to Hutton Castle. He was given no indication of what was to be discussed, only that he was to keep his journey confidential. On Burrell's informing him that he and Lady Burrell had decided to present the Collection to the City of Glasgow, Honeyman later recalled that he was too excited to be coherent. His reaction is scarcely to be wondered at; by that time Burrell's collection was already outstanding in the fields of Gothic Art, Oriental ceramics and bronzes, and nineteenth-century French painting. Its offer to Glasgow was, by any reckoning, staggeringly generous.

What finally led Burrell to offer the Collection to Glasgow was, as he said in a press interview at the time, his affection for the city of his birth. Another reason was his respect at that time for Tom Honeyman. In

May 1944 Burrell wrote that Honeyman's 'great knowledge of art was one of the principal factors which decided my wife and myself to offer our Collection to Glasgow'.

Once he had made up his mind Burrell wanted the matter settled as soon as possible and he demanded a decision from Glasgow Corporation before the end of January. Throughout the month a series of discussions took place on Burrell's insistence under conditions of secrecy between his solicitor, Tom Honeyman, the Town Clerk, the Convenor of the Art Galleries Committee and the Lord Provost. It may seem that the City officials were looking a gift horse in the mouth in not accepting the cornucopia immediately, but it was the terms and conditions which Burrell attached to the gift which rightly caused them to hesitate. Some were fairly minor and presented no difficulties, such as that the Hutton drawing-room, hall and dining room were to be reconstructed with their fittings and furnishings in the building that was to be built to house the Collection; also that this building was to contain only Burrell's collection and any additions to it made by Sir William and Lady Burrell and their daughter, or by the Trustees of the Collection. Other requirements were less welcome and one in particular was a major stumbling block. Burrell reiterated his long held belief that the Collection must be housed in a rural setting far removed from the atmospheric pollution of urban conurbations. More precisely, although it was agreed that the site for the building to house and display the Collection could be chosen by the Corporation (subject to the approval of Burrell and his wife or their testatory Trustees) this apparent freedom of action was drastically circumscribed by his insistence that this site must not be less than sixteen miles from the Royal Exchange in Glasgow and within four miles of Killearn in Stirlingshire. William Kerr, the Town Clerk, expressed his misgivings that post-war planning and development controls might well rule out all possible sites in such a rigidly specified and small area. Another factor which weighed heavily on the minds of the City officials was the difficulties in administrating the Collection so far away from Glasgow. Tom Honeyman took upon himself the unenviable task of trying to persuade Burrell to allow more flexibility in the siting of the Collection. Burrell's reaction was violent and Honeyman recorded that his proposal 'when it reached Hutton Castle . . . almost set the place on fire. The telephone buzzed for days.'

Burrell, determined as ever and in an impregnable position, would brook no tampering with his stipulations: it was simply a case of agreeing to them or losing the Collection. Honeyman firmly recommended acceptance and this the Corporation did, swallowing with difficulty Burrell's site terms. On 4 February Burrell was informed of the Corporation's decision and at the end of March a Memorandum of Agreement was signed by both parties. This of course included all Burrell's conditions, but they were made more palatable by his agreeing to make provision in his will for the construction costs of the building to house the Collection and make funds available for future acquisitions. The application of the latter sums was to be in the hands of his Trustees, although as regards additions to the Collection Sir William and Lady Burrell stated that 'a very decided preference [should] be given to works of the highest standard of the Gothic period'. The donees (i.e. the Corporation) were forbidden to sell, donate or exchange anything from the Collection, but temporary loans were permitted to publicly owned galleries in Great Britain. These loan terms, however, are surprisingly loosely drafted. Although the donors stated that prior to the erection of the building to house the Collection the textiles could not be exhibited within sixteen miles of the Glasgow Royal Exchange, the lending of tapestries, carpets and needlework, etc. to galleries in cities with the same air pollution problems as Glasgow was not prohibited. Moreover, although the Memorandum refers to loans to public galleries in Great Britain, the sending of items from the Collection to exhibitions abroad was not specifically excluded. It was also unclear whether Northern Ireland was included. Such points were only clarified in the course of time at the cost of much ill-feeling between Burrell and the senior management of Glasgow Museums and Art Galleries.

Not quite all Burrell's collection was to go to Glasgow. Items identified in a book of photographs were not considered suitable by Burrell and the gift also excludes a number of articles (all save one unspecified) which he intended to bequeath to certain other public collections in Great Britain. In the event only his 'local' art gallery at Berwick-on-Tweed was to benefit: in 1949 it received 42 paintings, mainly nineteenth-century French and Dutch pictures, including works by Boudin, Degas, Bosboom and James Maris.

In addition to the moveable objects which comprised the vast majority of the Collection the gift also included all the ancient architectural and sculptural stonework, including fireplaces, and wooden doors and stained glass which Burrell had incorporated into the fabric of Hutton Castle. The donors did not intend that Hutton should continue in private domestic use after their deaths and the Memorandum envisaged that it might become a publicly owned institution of some kind. The removal of the built-in items in the event left Hutton a gutted shell; possibly Burrell realised that Lorimer had been right in his adverse judgement on the Castle (although he never admitted it) and that a fresh start could be made on a new gallery utilising the best features from Hutton. He certainly intended that they would have a strong influence on the eventual appearance of the new gallery and on this subject Burrell expressed himself unequivocally in the Memorandum. In addition to wanting the drawing-room, dining room and hall from Hutton reconstructed, he and Lady Burrell stated:

> . . . the Collection as far as possible be shown as it would be in a private house e.g. . . . the tapestries, furniture, beds etcetera should be placed in rooms throughout the building with appropriate furniture so as to ensure that the building has as little resemblance to a Museum as possible.

One way and another the Memorandum of Agreement severely hampered the freedom of action of both the recipients of Burrell's collection and his Trustees. By the time the Agreement was signed he was already 82 and did not expect to see many more days; he was determined that both the site and layout of the building should reflect his own views, even if he did not live to see it. He could not have foreseen the difficulties that his conditions were to create for all concerned, and especially for himself. Instead of being able to spend the twilight of his life in peace, secure in the knowledge that the future of the Collection was assured, Burrell had to endure bitter wrangles and disappointments.

At least the immediate aftermath of the conclusion of the Agreement was gratifying for him. Press and public reaction was very favourable and he was widely praised for his generosity. Furthermore Glasgow Corporation acknowledged his public-spiritedness by granting him the freedom of the city. But even in 1944 the storm clouds which were to mar the relationship between the old man and the rulers of his birthplace were already gathering.

6

THE LAST YEARS

Sir William mentioned . . . that he had stopped 'buying'. If this is true . . . well . . . he has not done too badly!
                                        Murray Adams-Acton

SIR William Burrell lived for another fourteen years after the completion of the negotiations over the gift of his collection to Glasgow. In appearance he remained as upright as he had in his younger days, but as the years progressed he became increasingly gaunt through a combination of advanced age and his diet, which was more spartan than ever. The impression he gave to the end was formidable. On being asked to describe Burrell, one of his last visitors replied that he was too much in awe of him even to look at him. Yet he retained to the end his sense of humour. In his mid-nineties, Burrell described his health as 'like a faulty electric point: I never know when I am going to flicker and go out and when I am going to work'. His constitution was by nature robust and although inevitably he suffered bouts of infirmity, by husbanding his resources he enjoyed remarkably good health at least until the last two or three years of his life. Burrell and his wife were too frail to resume the West Indies cruises and the buying expeditions to Paris and elsewhere in Europe which they had so much enjoyed in the pre-war years, but they still travelled frequently within England and Scotland. They did not stint on accommodation, staying at hotels like the Grosvenor in London and the Cavendish at Eastbourne. They tended as the years went by to confine their holidays to the north. In 1949 and 1951 they only went a short distance down the Northumberland coast to Seahouses and in 1953 to Edinburgh, although as late as May 1955 they ventured as far south as London and Hythe. Occasionally Burrell went through to Glasgow, usually to view

exhibitions of his collection, such as that held in the McLellan Galleries in 1949.

He remained mentally alert to the end. In the 1940's the officials of Glasgow Museums and Art Galleries were inundated with letters on a variety of topics to do with the Collection. Rarely a day went by without a communication from Hutton Castle arriving on the desk of either Tom Honeyman or Andrew Hannah, and two letters a day were by no means uncommon. It must have been with a feeling of some weariness, not to say trepidation, that these epistles were opened. In the years after the end of the war much of the correspondence was concerned with arrangements for the transfer to Kelvingrove of those items on loan

Civic honour — Sir William signs the Visitors' Book in the presence of his wife and Lord Provost Welsh at City Chambers on the occasion of his receiving the Freedom of the City of Glasgow in 1944.

throughout the British Isles and at Hutton. The details were so precisely worked out by Burrell that a hitch rarely occurred. A constant worry in his mind was that the Collection was being properly maintained by Glasgow Museums and Art Galleries, and he wrote a number of letters giving advice on storage and conservation of tapestries, carpets and furniture. Events which caused a flood of letters from Hutton were the 1945, 1949 and 1951 exhibitions of the Burrell Collection in Kelvingrove and the McLellan Galleries. Burrell involved himself in these shows wholeheartedly, especially with regard to the display of the European, Near Eastern and Chinese ceramics and Chinese bronzes. His letters contained suggestions for themes and even rough sketches of individual case layouts.

Burrell's mental powers may have remained as sharp as ever but in his declining years he became prey as do so many old people to certain fears and obsessions. During the early stages of the Second World War, the progress of which he followed closely and on which he quite often commented to Drake and Honeyman, he became worried that the Germans would confiscate his collection if they invaded and conquered the United Kingdom. Some of the precautions taken, for instance the removal of the ancient stained glass from the windows at Hutton to preserve them from bomb damage, were sensible even if the prospects of an air raid in the vicinity of Hutton were remote; others were excessive, such as the detaching of all the photographs of his collection from the albums in which they were mounted and identified. He even went so far as to burn a mass of letters concerning various acquisitions, a course of action we have cause to regret today, especially as he steadfastly resisted all attempts to record his memoirs as a collector.

In the 1950's theft of his treasures at Hutton replaced the menace of invasion as Burrell's principal concern. The police constable based at Paxton was constantly called out to investigate complaints that he was being cheated or that the house was under threat from burglars. Two or three years before Burrell died the threat materialised and there was an attempted break-in. The old man heard the would-be intruders trying to enter the castle and fired both barrels of a shotgun from his bedroom window in the general direction of the sounds. Fortunately he succeeded in both missing and deterring the burglars. Subsequently Burrell installed bars in front of the ground floor windows, an exercise which was demonstrated to be useless by the local bobby who gained direct access to the first floor rooms by using the bars as ladders. He got no thanks for proving that they were a waste of money.

A melancholic strain manifested itself in the last years. On several occasions Burrell bemoaned lost opportunities in collecting and his bad luck. In 1942 he described a French fourteenth-century stained-glass panel depicting St John the Baptist, which he had bought at auction from the Mortimer Schiff Collection, as 'the first real bargain I have had for a considerable time'. He was correct in calling it a bargain – it cost the ridiculously small sum of £49 18s, including Drake's commission. In the same year he told Honeyman that he had purchased Monticelli's *The Bazaar, Marseilles,* a picture he had owned many years before and had sold: 'I had a great stroke of luck recently – the first for many years – and it has given me great pleasure.' *See plate 24*

By nature a conservative and patriot, the political scene in post-war Britain depressed him greatly and he expressed his views forcibly to Wilfred Drake: 'There are too many dreamers, visionaries & fatheads in this Country & but for that fact this war would never have occurred' (Burrell to Drake 8.5.45). '... the world is still too full of unrest and we are evidently intent on throwing away India as we have done Southern Ireland and Egypt' (Burrell to Drake 15.12.45). As might be expected, he had no confidence in the Labour Government of 1945 and for a short while after it took power even contemplated curtailing his buying.

Burrell was never an easy man with whom to live and the strains on his family must have been particularly difficult in his last years. Certainly he did not mellow with age and he remained as implacable and unforgiving as ever when faced with opposition to his own views. There were a number of individuals and institutions who now joined Joseph Duveen, Robert Lorimer and others who had fallen from grace and were condemned by Burrell to life-long emnity with no prospect of remission. Included amongst them were those critics and art historians who dared to question the authenticity of items in his collection and, by implication, his judgement. Doubts raised about the Bellini *Virgin and* *See plate 1* *Child* and a large early-sixteenth century French limestone statue of St Martha aroused his scorn. Regarding the former he wrote to Honeyman enclosing newspaper cuttings:

> As you know there are always 'wise ones' going about who doubt the authenticity of every other picture and evidently the Bellini did not escape them but these articles are useful as showing how these gentlemen went wrong.

The attack on the St Martha led to a more heated denunciation:

> Amongst the items at the Exhibition [the McLellan Galleries show of 1949] stated to be spurious by the gentleman from London was the life-size statue of Saint Marthe. . . . There is always a crop of 'critics' who consider they are placing themselves above their fellows & creating a favourable impression for themselves by damning exhibits. Instead of which they are completely giving themselves away & losing any reputation they might have. It is a type & there are many of them.

It must be said that in both instances Burrell's faith has been vindicated by subsequent researches.

The recipient of these observations was Tom Honeyman, who himself fell from favour. In many respects the deterioration of Honeyman's relations with Burrell was a repeat of Lorimer's experiences. Honeyman, like Lorimer, was a strong personality who was not afraid to express his opinions and did not possess (or was not prepared to employ) that ability to combine deference with gentle persuasion which Frank Surgey and Wilfred Drake found essential to cultivate in order to maintain good relations with Burrell. He was never a man to whom one could dictate and have his wishes and opinions ignored or questioned. Honeyman, like Lorimer before him, committed these mortal sins.

It will be recalled that in 1944 Tom Honeyman was very much in Burrell's confidence and had been instrumental in securing the gift of his collection for Glasgow. The first signs of a cooling in their friendship came at the end of the following year when Burrell replied to a letter of Honeyman in which he had passed an adverse opinion on nine of Matthew Maris' pictures in the Collection. Burrell reacted strongly, not only enclosing books on the artist by Friedländer and Croal Thomson but laboriously copying out long extracts from them. The letter covers four foolscap pages and ends:

> You write 'Each of these (9) pictures is, in my judgment, unworthy of exhibition because of their present state. They are not all equally bad but I very much doubt if any cleaning or restoration will restore any of them to their original quality. Their present condition is not due to neglect but to something inherent in the pictures'. Some day I hope you may change your opinion.

Burrell signed off 'Yours faithfully' instead of the 'Yours sincerely' of earlier correspondence, the same indication of growing disapproval which Lorimer had received nearly half a century before. Burrell was nothing if not consistent.

No other bone of contention appeared between the two men for a few years, although their earlier intimacy was not restored. Then in 1949–50 several issues arose which led to a more-or-less complete breakdown of the relationship. The first concerned Burrell's gift of pictures to Berwick-on-Tweed. The inclusion of a Daubigny and a Degas was strongly resisted by Honeyman:

> There is not the slightest doubt in my mind that the Daubigny which you have selected for Berwick is the best example of this artist's work in the Burrell Collection . . . and I think it would be lamentable if the finest example of his work were taken from the Burrell Collection. With regard to the Degas, I am in the course of preparing an article 'Degas in the Burrell Collection', and a featured point in that article will be the extraordinary range of Degas of different kinds, one way or another, assembled by one collector in his lifetime. Even the removal of a sketch from this group weakens the argument. On the level of scholarship it is of infinitely greater value to keep these pictures together than to

have one isolated at Berwick. To sum up and with the utmost respect I do insist that the removal of these two particular items weakens the Burrell Collection . . . and I very seriously ask you to reconsider again these two items.

In the face of such a direct challenge Burrell's response was not to budge, but the tone of his reply was for him mild. He explained that he had only bought the Daubigny as an exchange for a picture he had returned to a dealer:

> The Daubigny was the only respectable picture he had & I took it, not because I would otherwise have bought it, but to save my money. The Degas is only a sketch and you have 17 left including the best picture he ever painted. . . .

Honeyman had no option but to accede to Burrell's wishes, but unwisely he did so with a bad grace:

> I shall advise the Committee that this must be done and record what I have already said regarding the Degas and the Daubigny. I regret that my opinion expressed with conviction and a desire to be of help is considered once again to be valueless. I shall take care not to offer it again.

This prompted Burrell to invoke the earlier dispute over Matthew Maris:

> I have your letter of 11th and note that you are recording your views about the Degas and the Daubigny. At the same time I shall be glad if you will also place on record the fact that you requested me to take back five [sic – it should be nine] beautiful pictures by Matthew Maris.

Just over a year later there was an acrimonious exchange of correspondence about the siting of the new building to house the Collection. It seems to have originated in a mis-interpretation by Burrell of a report by Honeyman, but the tone adopted by both parties shows how little trust there was between them. Burrell quoted part of Honeyman's report in which he had stated that the Burrell Collection gallery should form part of a larger scheme.

> I am amazed at this expression of opinion on your part. It clearly means that you wish to upset the Agreement . . . *but that will not be done.* My wife and I will never agree to any alteration in the Agreement. . . .

Honeyman explained that what he meant was that the building should be set in a park which also had education and recreational facilities. His letter ended with an expression of exasperation:

> I think it better that I should not harass you with further communications as it seems clear that I do not possess your confidence since so often comments on my part lead you to believe that my motives are ulterior.

From this point onwards few letters were exchanged directly between Burrell and Honeyman, both men preferring to convey their views and wishes via Andrew Hannah. This did not prevent further bad feelings. Later in 1950 a minor dispute arose between Hannah and Burrell over the sum of money allotted for purchases from the interest on the sum invested for the new building, and Hannah asked Honeyman to help sort it out. Foreseeing that this was the sort of issue which could escalate out of control Honeyman declined to become involved. It did him no good in Burrell's eyes for soon afterwards he wrote to Hannah on another matter:

> Will you please explain to Dr Honeyman that his help was not required then and is not required now.

The last flare-up between the two, again conducted through Hannah, took place in 1953. This time the fault was entirely Honeyman's. Burrell discovered that Honeyman had in cavalier fashion disregarded his prohibition on loans from the Collection outside the British Isles and lent two paintings to a gallery in Winterthur, Switzerland. The wording of the Memorandum of Agreement on the subject of loans is imprecise, but Burrell had made his intentions clear in subsequent correspondence with Honeyman. The result was a very angry letter from Burrell to Hannah in which he said that the Agreement must never be broken again. Had the issue arisen soon after the gift of the Collection and before the bulk of it had been transferred to Glasgow it is conceivable that Burrell would have cancelled the arrangement.

Honeyman may have taken some small comfort from the fact that he was not the only target of the old man's wrath. Another was not an individual, but the city of Edinburgh. This episode was touched upon in the last chapter. In the early 1940's the civic authorities there had the responsibility of collecting iron in the area for use in the war effort, but the idea became fixed in Burrell's mind that ornamental railings and gates were excluded. Consequently when those surrounding Hutton were removed he was outraged, and even more so by the offer of £3 as compensation. The estimated cost for replacing them was £640 and Burrell therefore considered that he had lost well over £600. This of course hit him where it hurt most and he harped on about it repeatedly. His attitude was that of an Old Testament prophet, and is summed up in one of his letters on the subject: '. . . in this world there are few games that have not got a return match'. For the rest of his life he refused every request from Edinburgh for loans of items from the Collection, saying that he would not change his attitude until he received the cost of replacing his railings.

In the last years of his life Burrell's habitual penny-pinching became obsessive. Most of the many stories recounted about his miserliness date from this period. Some can be verified, others are apocryphal or have become exaggerated in the telling. One of those which is based on reliable evidence concerns a visit made to the premises of a dealer to settle a bill which was about to be sent to him. After he left the proprietor discovered that he had removed the unfranked $2\frac{1}{2}$d stamp from the envelope containing the bill.

Many of these quirks of behaviour can be put down to an old man's fetish. Moreover it tends to be overlooked that he was still capable of acts of kindness and generosity. His Jekyll and Hyde attitude to money is well illustrated by a dinner party held in Glasgow to celebrate the second exhibition of the Burrell Collection, which took place in the McLellan Galleries in 1951. Amongst Burrell's guests were John and Gertrude Hunt, and a German white wine of a particular vintage was served which Burrell had had, at considerable expense, sent up from London because he remembered from pre-war days that it was Mrs Hunt's favourite. On another occasion Burrell tried hard to obtain a better position for a gardener who had left his service eighteen years before.

Apart from the gift of his collection to Glasgow, a number of other public bodies were recipients of Burrell's munificence. At Hutton he performed the local squire's traditional good works, presenting a community hall to the village. On a much larger scale he gave the Glasgow Cancer Hospital the sum of £10,000 to purchase radium. Furthermore when in 1946 he became the recipient of the St Mungo Prize, awarded triennially to the individual who has done most for the good of the city of Glasgow, he handed the entire sum of £1,000 to various West of Scotland charities.

Tragically it was his greatest act of generosity, the donation of his art collection to Glasgow, which soured the last years of his life and left him embittered as well as rather lonely. The source of the trouble was the finding of a suitable site for the building to house the Collection. The matter lay dormant while both Glasgow Corporation and Burrell found their feet in the first years after the war. He had originally agreed to provide for the costs of the building in his will, but in 1946 he anticipated this by giving the Corporation £250,000 for this purpose; two years later he added another £200,000. It was shortly before the second donation that the search for a site began in earnest. From the outset Frank Surgey was heavily involved, on the strength of his work at Hutton twenty years earlier. He drew up preliminary plans and inspected potential locations in the Killearn area with Burrell and Corporation officials. Early runners were 'Whiteflat', Ballindalloch House and 300-acre estate near Balfron, Carbeth House, Balfunning House and Finnich Malice (near Drymen), the last then occupied by Dr O.H. Mavor *alias* James Bridie the playwright. In June 1948 the Sub-Committee of the Corporation detailed to find a site decided to open negotiations for either Ballindalloch or Finnich Malice. Progress was closely monitored by Burrell who gave some characteristically canny advice:

Don't be in a hurry. Time is on your side. Large houses today are worth next to nothing. . . . Cleverly managed you should get any one of these estates at the value of the land.

The discussions did not bear immediate fruit and led Hannah to report to Burrell in terms which were prophetic: '. . . in spite of our efforts to speed things up, it looks as if negotiations for a site might be rather protracted'. It is doubtful whether even Hannah at his most pessimistic envisaged that it would take another eighteen years before even a site was agreed, let alone have the Collection permanently housed and displayed.

In the event nothing came of the negotiations for any of these estates and after a brief flirtation with the Duke of Montrose's Buchanan Castle (disliked by Burrell on the grounds that it was 'a terribly wet place') attention turned to Mugdock Castle and its 300-acre estate, in the possession of the wealthy store-owner Hugh Fraser. This appealed to Frank Surgey as it met his requirements for a building with period architecture which could be used as a nucleus (Mugdock consists of a house of *c*.1875 with considerable remains of a medieval castle). Mugdock is near Milngavie and well within the proscribed sixteen mile radius of Glasgow. Nonetheless Burrell agreed with some reluctance that it could be considered. Surgey came up from the south to inspect it and in September 1949 wrote optimistically to Hannah:

Sir William is now prepared to have the museum outside the prescribed area if I can recommend a site with substantial advantages over any of the sites in the Killearn area.

He repeated this statement to Honeyman and went on to say:

I think he [Burrell] would give it his blessing if it was advantageous for the people of Glasgow to have a museum within easy reach of the city.

In his desire to see a site chosen before he died Burrell was therefore considering altering the terms of his gift, but he was an old man and needed to be handled delicately. At this very moment the worst that could happen did happen, for the Corporation decided to make a direct approach to him to relax the conditions. It was one thing making up his own mind, it was quite another having a second party trying to do it for him. Burrell reacted in characteristically stubborn fashion and dug his heels in. For some months relations between him and the Corporation remained poor and, as Hannah told Surgey, he was inclined to view any suggestion with suspicion, including Mugdock. Eventually Burrell was prevailed upon to have another look at this site and early in 1951 he gave it his consent. The proposal to purchase the estate for the purpose of building a museum to house the Burrell Collection was passed by the Corporation on 12 April and it looked as if the matter was at last resolved. It was, however, not to be, for negotiations with Hugh Fraser fell through. Almost immediately a potential saviour appeared on the scene in the shape of Mrs Therese Grabowsky Connell, the widow of a well-known Glasgow shipbuilder. She owned the Dougalston estate of 370 acres, quite near Mugdock Castle, and as she was prepared to donate it to the City of Glasgow the attraction was obvious. The difficulty was, as ever, in persuading Burrell. His first reactions were unfavourable, for he considered Dougalston less suitable than Mugdock as it was not in such a commanding position and was two miles nearer to Glasgow. The omens were therefore not good when the time came for an offical approach from the Corporation. The Convenor of the Glasgow Museums and Art Galleries Committee prepared a persuasive speech to try and overcome Burrell's resistance. In the event it remained undelivered, for Burrell concluded the meeting almost before it had began by saying, 'All right! I approve. And I am very hungry. When do we have lunch?' The original stipulations about the site were amended and in October came the announcement that Mrs Connell was presenting the house and estate to Glasgow in memory of her husband. The gift was made subject to her retaining a life interest and on condition that a building would be constructed there to display the Burrell Collection.

Even though building could not start until after Mrs Connell's death the Corporation was extraordinarily dilatory in settling the exact site on the estate. A list of suggested locations was prepared but it was not until November 1954 that the Committee inspected them. Even then no firm decision was made as it transpired that Mrs Connell had her own views which differed from those of the Corporation officials.

In the meantime quite independently and unbeknown to each other the former partners in Acton Surgey Ltd, Murray Adams-Acton and Frank Surgey, submitted schemes for the new building to Burrell for his

Dougalston. The gift of this house and estate by Mrs Connell to Glasgow at long last seemed to have resolved the problem of siting the Collection. It was not to be, for the threat of mining by the National Coal Board was enough for Burrell to withdraw his approval.

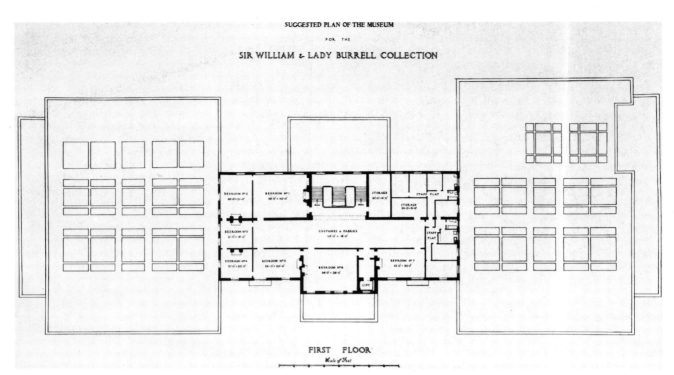

FIRST FLOOR
Scale of Feet

*Rival schemes by former partners.
The designs by Frank Surgey
(on this page) and Adams-Acton
(pages 164 and 165) for the gallery
to house the Burrell Collection.*

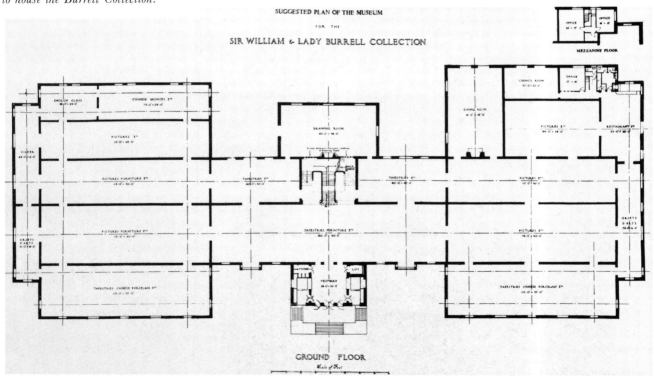

GROUND FLOOR
Scale of Feet

approval. Surgey had the advantage through knowing Burrell better and through his long involvement in the various negotiations for the site. Adams-Acton, on the other hand, had recently sold Burrell some large pieces of architectural stonework, including doorways and windows, from Hearst's collection; these were sufficiently monumental to affect the layout of any new building and Adams-Acton included them in his design.

The two schemes are very different. Frank Surgey's consists of an H-shaped structure with two large wings linked by a narrow central block. The wings are single-storey with the central section rising another floor to include the bedrooms from Hutton Castle. No items from the Collection are located and the ground floor galleries are plain rectangles. According to Mrs Surgey the elevation was to be neo-classical in style. Although elevation details of Adams-Acton's designs (he submitted three variants) are not specified the ground plans suggest that he too envisaged them as neo-classical. Here the similarities between the designs end. Adams-Acton opted for a centrally-planned structure with a series of galleries on two floors grouped around a courtyard which would contain flowers and trees (he was a very keen gardener). Whereas Surgey planned his galleries mainly in terms of a mixture of tapestries, paintings and Chinese porcelain, with smaller rooms for Chinese bronzes, *objets d'art*, silver and table glass, Adams-Acton in his third scheme adopted a sequence of period rooms and two picture galleries. He also indicated precise locations for individual objects, especially tapestries and furniture, as well as the architectural stonework.

Neither suggestion is very satisfactory, although in fairness it must be said that they were preliminary ideas and neither Surgey nor Adams-Acton was working to a detailed brief. Insufficient space is allotted for storage and offices and not enough attention is paid to consideration of lighting problems. Moreover whilst Surgey ignored the stained glass, Adams-Acton neglected the Chinese ceramics and bronzes and Oriental rugs.

It would be interesting to know what Burrell thought of the two schemes. There are, however, no recorded comments on Surgey's submission and only a few general remarks on Adams-Acton's work addressed to Hannah (typically the only aspect Burrell discussed with Adams-Acton directly was that of payment, which peeved the latter considerably):

> It places practically everything we have bought from him & I think places them well and that I consider to be of the highest importance.

Burrell continued:

> I like *very much* his idea of having a quadrangle *gay with flowers* . . .

Adams-Acton's designs incorporated the medieval stonework recently purchased from the Hearst Collection.

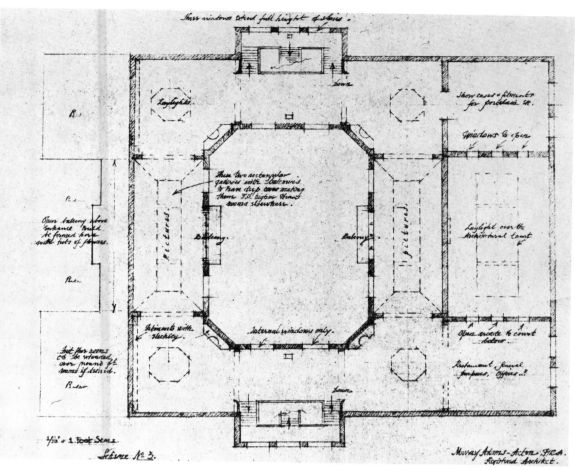

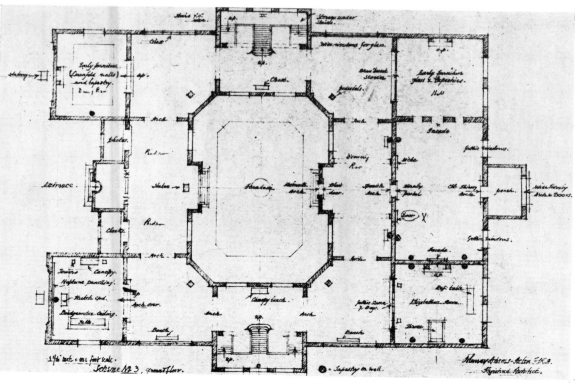

and I entirely agree with him that 'this place can be more attractive and unlike any other museum anywhere'.

Apart from this Burrell gave few indications that he had given the design of the building to house his collection serious consideration. In 1949 Hannah told Surgey that he thought Burrell favoured a structure which was thoroughly modern in appearance rather then a medieval or Elizabethan reconstruction. Burrell also stated that:

> The Museum, as stipulated in the deed of gift, should be as *simple as possible*. . . . To put up an extravagant building is quite opposed to what we have stipulated. What we need is fine contents.

It is a matter of conjecture whether either of the Adams-Acton or Surgey schemes would have satisfied Burrell had they been adopted: almost certainly there would have been the same wrangles that bedevilled the alterations to Hutton Castle. In the event both Adams-Acton and Surgey were spared. The Corporation was at long last on the point of announcing an architectural competition when disaster struck. In March 1955 Hannah, already dispirited by the continuous delays and procrastination, had to steel himself to inform Burrell that the National Coal Board was planning to sink shafts in the Dougalston area. This was sufficient for the old man to rescind the agreement and it was back to square one. Mrs Connell died a few months later and for a time Dougalston House was used as a store for part of the Collection. The Corporation spent considerable sums on its maintenance, but the property was never again considered as a possible site for the new gallery and in February 1975 it was returned to Mrs Connell's trustees. Ironically, the threatened mining development has never materialised.

The failure of the Dougalston project must have been shattering for Burrell, especially as he had every reason to hope that the exact site and design for the building to house the Collection would be settled before he died. Notwithstanding this blow and in spite of his great age (he was 93 at the time Dougalston was eliminated) he returned energetically to the pursuit of Mugdock. Bill Wells, who was appointed Keeper of the Burrell Collection in January 1956, remembers Burrell leaping out of the bed to which he was by then almost permanently confined to go downstairs and telephone Hugh Fraser. The negotiations were as fruitless as the previous round had been and when Burrell died the Collection was still without a permanent home.

However great his frustrations over the site for the building, Burrell could always find consolation in collecting. Between 1944 and 1957 additions were made which in certain areas raised their importance to the first rank. In this period the Collection grew at an even faster rate than before, with more than two thousand objects added to the original gift. This total includes nearly three hundred items such as knives, tea-sets, stained glass and a Phil May sketchbook which were donated in 1951 by Sir William and Lady Burrell, but the remainder were all purchased. In several years, notably 1947 and 1948, the number of acquisitions exceeded those for any single pre-war year. The figures are as follows:

1944 : 88	1951 : 51 (excluding the gifts made this year)
1945 : 204	1952 : 93
1946 : 289	1953 : 73
1947 : 616	1954 : 72
1948 : 726	1955 : 50
1949 : 82	1956 : 34
1950 : 151	1957 : 26

For Burrell the art world at the end of the war was very different from that which it had been in 1939. His advanced years precluded buying forays to Paris and even his pre-war group of trusted agents and advisers did not survive long. Wilfred Drake died in 1948, Frank Partridge in 1952 and Frank Surgey, after a brief return to the antique business, took up farming, although as we have seen he continued to be consulted about the site for the Collection. The Hunts too had bought a farm in 1938 by Lough Gur in County Limerick, where John had spent his early years. After the war they both renewed their art dealing and were frequently in London, but as they remained based in Ireland they lost the close contact with Burrell they had formerly enjoyed; nevertheless he did purchase some things from them. In Ireland Hunt devoted most of his time to the study and collection of Irish antiquities, which a few years before his death in 1976 he presented to the State. To fill the gaps in the ranks Burrell turned to fresh recruits, but none ever enjoyed with him the degree of confidence of the afore-mentioned. There were also a number of important transactions with Murray Adams-Acton regarding the Hearst Collection, as we shall see presently.

There are certain changes in Burrell's pattern of buying compared with the pre-war years. He had never been an indiscriminate collector but had concentrated on particular fields, albeit far-spread ones, which appealed to his taste: nineteenth-century French and Dutch painting, later Chinese ceramics, and North European Late Gothic art, to name the most important. In the last thirteen years of his collecting he did not neglect these areas but tended to concentrate on aspects of the Collection which he considered needed strengthening in order to make it more comprehensive. He stated his policy on several occasions: 'I think it is better to fill the gaps than bid for better specimens of what we already have.' At the end of the war he gave priority to building up the early Chinese ceramics, bronzes and jades (up to 1945 there are only three *See plate 25* jades entered in the Purchase Books). The totals of ceramic purchases for the years 1944 to 1948 indicate the scale of the exercise:

1944 : 42   1947 : 122
1945 : 146   1948 : 130
1946 : 154

Although these figures included many items of the ubiquitous seventeenth and eighteenth-century polychrome wares there were a large number of much earlier pieces, from the Han, Tang, Song and early Ming dynasties. In 1944 and 1948 Burrell purchased a splendid series of Neolithic period wares from the N.S. Brown Collection which enabled him to inform Hannah both triumphantly and accurately, '. . . you will now have the largest collection of these in Britain'. The prices were as low as £11 and contrast with the huge sum (for Burrell) of £3,045 he paid in 1945 for a *famille noire* vase and pair of beakers at the important R.W.M. Walker Collection Sale. At the end of 1948 Burrell concluded that the Chinese section of the Collection was virtually complete and thereafter the additions are sporadic and come to a total halt in 1952. By then he had succeeded in forming one of the most important collections of Chinese art in the British Isles.

In 1947 and 1948 he also turned his attention to an area into which he had not ventured since 1921 and even before then had only dabbled: Persian and Turkish pottery and metalwork. In March 1947 Burrell wrote to Hannah on the subject of Turkish Iznik ware pottery: 'If this little programme could be carried out it would make this part of the collection more complete and more educative.' The 'little programme' was executed so quickly that five months later Burrell could tell Hannah, 'I think I have sufficient Rhodian [Iznik] now to fill a case and nearly enough Jade for another – Also sufficient Persian items for a case.' Altogether 161 pieces of Persian and Iznik pottery and eight items of Persian metalwork were acquired in these two years; Persian ceramics continued to flow into the Collection at a steady rate to the end. In the same letter Burrell also said, 'The Egyptian and the Greek items I am short in but if I am spared I hope to complete them.' He was indeed spared and from 1947 onwards until the Purchase Books came to an end ten years later it was the Ancient Civilisations section which enjoyed the largest number of acquisitions. Not just of Egyptian and Greek artefacts but also many from Mesopotamia, Assyria, Etruria and Rome. With the exception of four Egyptian pieces Burrell had shown no interest in this field before 1945, but now he formed considerable holdings: there are in the Collection today nearly three hundred artefacts from Ancient Egypt, two hundred Greek and Etruscan items and about a hundred Roman objects. Even smaller in quantity are the Sumerian pieces (approximately sixty), the Assyrian objects (twelve) and the Luristan bronzes (about forty). These last three categories have an importance out of all proportion to the number of objects. The Luristan bronzes are a particularly interesting collection and the

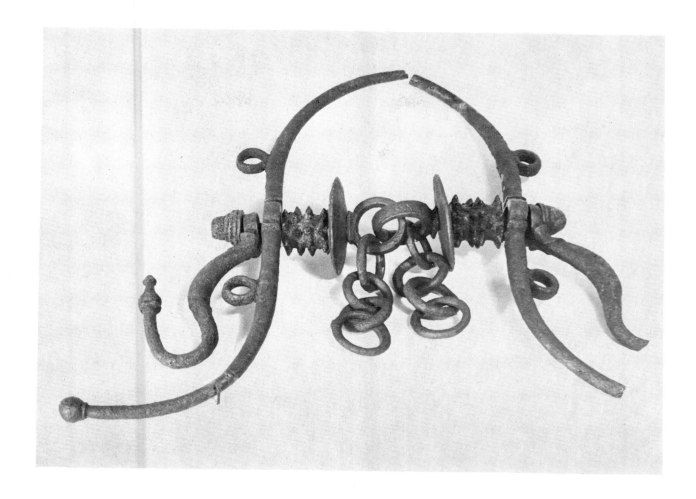

Etruscan bronze horse bit, c. 500 BC.

Assyrian pieces chiefly comprise a number of fragments of reliefs from the great palace complexes at Nimrud and Nineveh. Most of these reliefs are very small and were inexpensive, but the largest, a profile head, cost Burrell £1,000 when he bought it from Spink's on 18 June 1947. On the same occasion he paid £4,500 for a bronze bust of Hermes said to have been found near Larissa in Thessaly and formerly in the collection of Viscount Tredegar. The vast majority of the Ancient Civilisations aquisitions consisted of pottery and stone vessels, glass and small bronze ceramic cult figures, and were obtained for modest prices.

It has to be said that this area together with the Persian ceramics shows a falling-off in quality compared with the remainder of the Collection. One reason for this lies in the fact that it was a field already well-harvested by earlier collectors and there were few rich gleanings to be had. Other factors were Burrell's old age and his methods of collecting. He was, naturally enough, not quite as discriminating as he had been and in addition he was sailing into seas which for him were almost

New pastures in Burrell's last years: the bronze bust of Hermes reputedly found in Thessaly. His haggling reduced the price from £6,000 to £4,500.

entirely uncharted: in this respect it is interesting that at the end of the 1953 Purchase Books are a few brief notes on aspects of Ancient Egyptian life. These handicaps were compounded by the fact that contrary to his pre-war practice of buying individual pieces after careful personal inspection, now he tended to make purchases in bulk at auctions (with dealers bidding on his behalf) and direct from the trade. Whenever possible he still came to London and had items sent on approval to Hutton, but frequently he was forced to rely on a photograph or take the vendor's word. In most instances he was treated fairly, but there were a number of objects purchased in these years which are not all what they were presented as being, either because they are not of ancient date or because they have been excessively restored. It is true that Burrell was also buying Chinese ceramics and bronzes in similar fashion (there can scarcely have been a major sale in London of Chinese art between 1945 and 1948 at which he did not make acquisitions) but he was on surer ground here as he knew the subject better and was relying on individuals with whom he had done business for many years. Wherever possible he continued his pre-war practice of asking for a second opinion, and if it was unfavourable he returned the piece in question or sold it. Referring to three Egyptian items he said:

> . . . I am anxious that the Collection should be as [free] as possible of anything that may not be quite right.

The Purchase Books and correspondence files contain a number of references to items weeded out in this fashion, but by no means all of them are of the Ancient Civilisations. Burrell lacked someone in this field to do his vetting of the calibre of Professor Yetts, who examined his Chinese bronzes in 1948: much to Burrell's satisfaction Yetts gave the vast majority a clean bill of health, although two were declared to be fakes and were sent for sale at Christie's.

'You get what you pay for' is a truism which is particularly applicable to the art world and Burrell was on occasions prepared to pay very large sums indeed for works of art of high quality. Even though in the last years his attention centred on Chinese art and Ancient Civilisations, it was, as ever, the more familiar paintings and tapestries which were his most expensive purchases. In 1946 Burrell acquired at the Viscount Rothermere Sale the Rembrandt *Self-Portrait* of 1632; the price paid, including Partridge's commission for bidding, was £13,125. This was the largest sum he had laid out so far for a single work of art, but it was exceeded two years later by the *Portrait of a Gentleman* *See plate 26* attributed to Frans Hals, which cost £14,500. In at least two instances Burrell had to pay considerable amounts for items he had tried to acquire before the war. The first of these was the German tapestry altar *See plate 27* frontal depicting the Holy Trinity which he had attempted to buy in 1928 at the Sir Hercules Read Sale. It fetched £4,200 on that occasion, and in 1946 Burrell had to bid £5,400, excluding dealer's commission, in order to secure it. It should be borne in mind, however, that in terms of real purchasing power the pound was worth less in 1945 than in 1928: it has been estimated that £5,400 is the equivalent of under £3,000 in 1928. The second acquisition was the splendid series of 39 sixteenth-century panels of heraldic glass from Fawsley Hall in Northamptonshire depicting the arms and alliances of the Knightley family. The saga of the Fawsley glass is a lengthy one and is an excellent example of Burrell's patience and determination when he came across something he badly wanted.

The story began in August 1938 when Drake, almost certainly with Burrell in mind as a prospective purchaser, offered Viscount Gage £1,000 for the set. Gage's agents replied that they would obtain an expert opinion before accepting or rejecting the offer, but subsequently there was silence. A year later Drake wrote again, raising the sum by £100 to include the five shields with the Washington family arms in the parish church of Fawsley. At the outbreak of war Drake withdrew his offer and in December wrote to Burrell hazarding a guess that as the hostilities showed no signs of an early conclusion Gage would be prepared to consider a lower offer. Burrell was very keen to have the glass and taking Drake's advice reduced the bid to £700. This was not accepted and after another attempt in 1941 the matter lay dormant for several years. Burrell did not forget it and not long after the war ended consulted Drake. Negotiations were still in progress when Drake died in 1948. Not long afterwards Tom Honeyman became involved. In July of the following year Burrell wrote to him:

> . . . I hope you will be successful in securing the Fawsley glass. As I mentioned the 39 pieces are worth on an average over £100 each namely £3900. . . .

In the end the series was acquired through the agency of Drake's partner Roy Grosvenor Thomas for £2,000, twice the amount it might have cost in 1938 had the matter been concluded then, but still a very good price for what is one of the finest sets of English armorial glass in existence. Moreover the Fawsley panels did not cost Burrell a penny. A few months earlier he had decided that because of the increase in death duties announced in the Budget he could no longer afford to pay for additions to the Collection from his own pocket. He came to an agreement with the Corporation whereby he was empowered to use for this purpose a proportion of the annual interest on the £450,000 he had given for the new museum. With his usual methodical fashion Burrell noted this arrangement after the 14 June entry in the 1949 Purchase Book:

> *Here end the Purchases by Sir William Burrell on his own account*

followed by

> *Purchases of the Glasgow Corporation.*

He also amended the format of the Purchase Books to take this into account.

As it happened the Fawsley glass was not paid for out of the interest on the building fund allocated to Burrell but after some heated exchanges, separately by the Corporation. However sensible the arrangement seemed in theory, in execution it was unsatisfactory to both parties and resulted in some unpleasant wrangles. These centred on whether Burrell was over-spending or whether he could carry over unspent sums from one year to the next; the issue was further complicated by the income he obtained from periodic sales of *objets d'art*, pictures, and modern jewellery. It was a thorny problem from both sides of the fence. Burrell found it difficult to accept that having made a gift of such a large sum of money it was no longer under his control; the Corporation officials, for their part, were obliged to ensure that the interest accruing was correctly applied. It was yet another cause of friction between Burrell and the City of Glasgow.

One consolation for the Corporation was that he was no more profligate with its money than he was with his own. He remained just as keen for a bargain after June 1949 as he had been before this date, and there were some very juicy plums indeed for the picking in the post-war years. Burrell's old failing of missing first-class acquisitions through a reluctance to pay the appropriate price occasionally still manifested itself. The most glaring instance of this was the large set of needlework

28 Some outstanding bargains in Oriental ceramics. The life-size Lohan (opposite page) dated AD 1484, purchased in 1944 for £350; and (left) the underglaze copper-red ewer of the late 14th century AD, which entered the Collection in 1947 for £85. These Chinese pieces are only surpassed in rarity by the Korean celadon bowl (right) bought in 1946 for £145.

29 One of Burrell's best acquisitions of medieval sculpture: the alabaster PIETÀ attributed to the Master of Rimini.

30 In store, 1981: a 14th-century window and an arch await their return to public gaze.

31 The positioning in January 1981 of the keystone of the great arch from Hornby Castle which forms the public entrance to the Collection.

wall-hangings from Oxburgh Hall in Norfolk embroidered by Mary Queen of Scots and her captor, the formidable Bess of Hardwick. The set was offered by the owners, the Bedingfield family, to Burrell for £10,000. He had the hangings on approval at Hutton but turned them down on the grounds that they had been so patched and restored that there was very little of the original work remaining. When in 1953 they were acquired by the Victoria and Albert Museum he wrote to Hannah stating that in his opinion they were not worth more than a few hundred pounds (and that for the historical association). There is a whiff of sour grapes about this letter, especially as Burrell refers in harsh terms to an individual concerned in the transaction who had not long before dared to question the authenticity of a number of items in the Collection.

The failure to obtain the Oxburgh Hall hangings is negligible when weighed against the magnificent range of additions made between 1944 and 1957. The first nine years in particular were a period of depressed prices in the London art market, brought about by a combination of national austerity, vigorous controls over the entry of foreign currency, poor purchasing power of the pound, and (between 1945 and 1951) a lack of confidence by collectors and dealers in the Labour Government. An additional factor was the absence from the market of the great American museums with their enormous financial resources.

The situation was appreciated perfectly by Burrell and he was not slow to take advantage, as is demonstrated by a letter written to Honeyman in 1945 regarding the *Jonathan* tapestry he had just purchased:

> The only important tapestry which has come on to the market for 8 or 10 years. When it was offered in Paris they asked £15,000 for it but the war has altered things – for the time being – in Paris. But they wont be long till they are at it again . . . Dr Kurth strongly urged me to buy it.

Dr Betty Kurth was the leading expert on medieval tapestries and was engaged by Burrell to write the catalogue of his collection; unfortunately she died before the task was completed. Burrell only paid £4,000 for this tapestry, which shows how low prices had fallen, especially when the decline in the purchasing power of the pound is taken into account. In the following year he was able to report the acquisition of a Chinese double gourd-shaped aubergine vase dating from the reign of the Emperor Wanli (AD 1573–1629) in similar tones of satisfaction:

> At one time it was bought by the great collector Raphael for £1280. But I got it much cheaper.

He did indeed – it only cost him £550. Burrell was as aware as ever of the depressed state of the art market a few years later, when shortly after the agreement had been made regarding the spending of part of the building fund interest he exhorted Honeyman in the following terms:

It would be . . . a thousand pities to miss fine additions, especially as they are becoming cheaper, on account of the lack of money.

The poor climate for vendors gave him the whip hand in his favourite game of haggling, although there can be little doubt that some dealers at least were wise to this and quoted prices knowing that they were going to have to settle for a lower figure. The Hermes bronze which as was mentioned above Burrell bought for £4,500 carried an initial price tag of £6,000. A Chinese jade of the Zhou dynasty obtained in 1948 was another victory for Burrell: 'The price was £395 & it was with the greatest difficulty I got it down to £300.' A letter written to Hannah reporting the acquisition at Sotheby's on 31 July 1951 of an English early sixteenth-century armet for £36 15s (including the usual 5% commission for his agent) shows that at the age of ninety he was alive as ever to the niceties of the art market:

It is worth at least £150 but the 31 July is the worst day of the year on which to sell i.e. the best day of the year on which to buy – most of the buyers having left London for the Moors – or holiday resorts.

As we have already seen, Burrell was quite prepared to pay very large sums on occasions, but these were few and far between. In the last ten or so years of his collecting he made some of the most successful forays of his entire career into the art market. Even though he burned his fingers with a number of the Ancient Civilisations and Near Eastern pieces these can be offset by several remarkable buys, including Sumerian items and the Assyrian palace reliefs. One particularly notable acquisition was an impressive bearded head in porphyry marble which entered the Collection in 1950. Scholarly opinion is divided on its date, the current view being that it is a Roman work of the first or second century AD. Whatever date it may be its superb quality makes the purchase price of £451 10s seem absurd. Even more staggering are some of the bargains Burrell obtained in Chinese ceramics, such as the

See plate 28

life-size glazed stoneware figure of a Lohan, dated AD 1484, which cost £350 in 1944, and a Han dynasty model of a three-storey building, for which he paid a mere £180 in the following year. This was a piece Burrell particularly admired, describing it as 'a wonderful thing'. This admiration is fully justified – it is a remarkable record of first-century Chinese architecture. Even these items pale into insignificance as regards price compared with a blue-and-white dish and an underglaze

See plate 28

copper-red ewer, both of the mid to late fourteenth century AD; they cost £60 and £85 respectively in 1945 and 1947, ridiculous sums compared with their present-day values, which are well into six figures. Alongside these should be placed a small Korean celadon bowl of the twelfth-thirteenth centuries AD, bought at the sale of the Marcus Ezekiel Collection on 3 June 1946 for £145. It is described in the

Catalogue as rare, but no-one at the time knew precisely how rare it is: there is only one other example of this type of ware in the British Isles and that is a damaged piece in the British Museum.

Equally remarkable were some of Burrell's purchases of European art of the fourteenth-sixteenth centuries. In addition to the tapestries mentioned above (and several others) two notable acquisitions of furniture were made: in 1946 he bought a well-known inlaid oak table dated 1569 and bearing the arms of the Brome and Crossley families. Only one other similar table is recorded, at Hardwick Hall in Derbyshire. Burrell purchased it for £1,675, which compares very favourably with the £2,750 he paid in 1924 for another Elizabethan inlaid table bearing the date 1567. For the second piece of furniture he was forced to bide his time. The Hunts had had since before the war in their country residence of Poyle Manor at Colnbrook in Buckinghamshire a splendid early sixteenth-century oak table with an elaborate trestle support and panelled in linenfold. This, like the *Bury Chest* mentioned in the last chapter, originally belonged to Durham Cathedral and stood in the kitchens in the monastic quarters (not the library as has long been thought). Burrell coveted this table very much but for years the Hunts resisted all his offers. Eventually in 1952, when they finally cleared Poyle, they reluctantly decided that it was too big to take to Ireland and let Burrell have it. He was delighted:

> I have bought a very important table which I have known about for years but which I didn't think would ever come our way as Mr Hunt steadfastly refused to sell . . . I have paid £2,025 for it plus the carriage London to Kelvingrove. . . .

Stained glass was another happy hunting-ground in this period. In 1946 he acquired through Wilfred Drake eight French early sixteenth-century panels with scenes from the life of St John the Baptist and four English armorial roundels from Blithfield Hall in Staffordshire, the residence of Lord Bagot. Burrell agreed initially with Drake to offer £1,500, including removal expenses, but in the end he secured them for as little as £850, which was increased by Drake's commission and the cost of removal and replacing the old glass to a final sum of £1,395 8s 9d. Once again, this was a very reasonable sum when compared with the windows he had purchased from Hearst's collection just before the war, and these were cheap enough.

The story of the Vale Royal acquisition is even by Burrell standards almost beyond belief. In February 1947 there appeared in Sotheby's salerooms a series of 37 armorial roundels and panels from Vale Royal in Cheshire. They were collected from various sources and include some outstanding examples of English sixteenth-century armorial glass; in terms of quality they rival the Fawsley series. As regards price

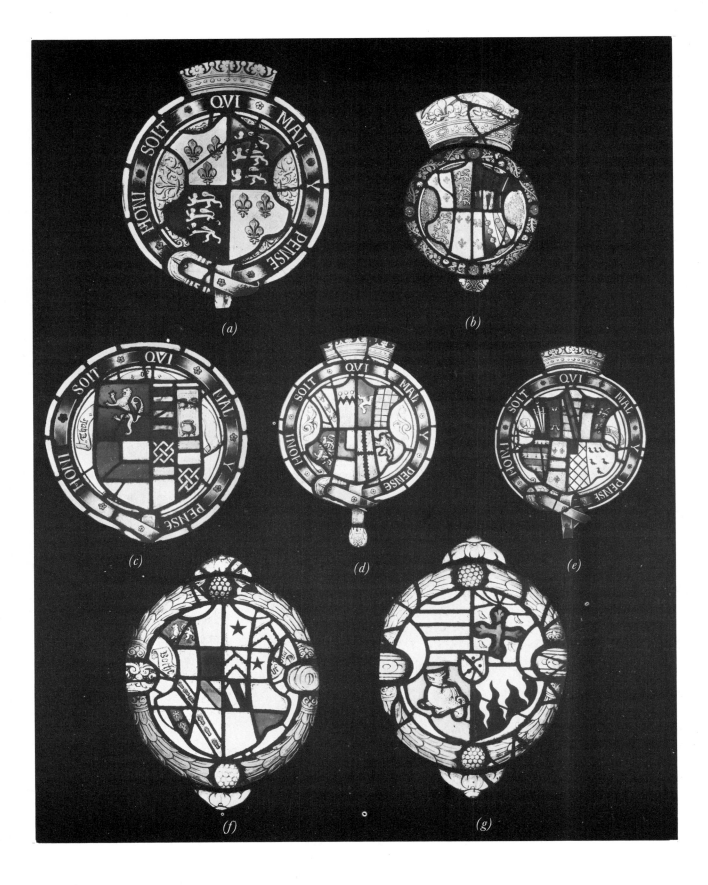

(a)   *(b)*

(c)   *(d)*   *(e)*

(f)   *(g)*

there is no comparison between the two, for Burrell succeeded in purchasing the Vale Royal glass for the negligible sum of £55, plus Drake's commission of £26, i.e. little more than £2 per panel. Burrell appreciated his good fortune and told Drake, 'I never thought you would get the glass for such a trifling sum.' It is particularly remarkable considering that a lot consisting of nineteenth-century glass in the same sale fetched £26, much to Burrell's scorn. It was with good reason that he paid tribute to Drake for his services over thirty years: 'Without you I could not have had so much good glass as you have enabled me to get.' It was probably for insurance purposes that the entry in the Purchase Books for the Vale Royal glass gives the price as £4,175.

Some of the best additions of medieval sculpture were made between 1952 and 1955, when the rate of acquisitions was declining. Amongst them were old favourites such as English alabaster panels; also a German early fourteenth-century marble statuette which is closely related to a series on the high altar of Cologne Cathedral, and an attractive alabaster *Pietà*, attributed to an unknown sculptor of the early fifteenth century known as the Master of Rimini. The purchase price of £175 for the *Pietà* may be compared with the £25,000 paid in 1978 for a similar piece in the Robert von Hirsch Collection. Larger in scale is the Spanish tomb effigy of Don Ramon, Baron de Espés bought in 1953 for £900. The price pleased Burrell:

> It is a wonderful thing to have secured. I got it just in time. Had it been English it would have fetched £3,000 to £4,000.

The tomb originally stood in the monastery church of St Maria de Obarra at Calvera near Huesca. Although it has suffered some restoration most of the original polychrome is intact.

Burrell showed great boldness in the acquisition of a series of items of architectural stonework and woodwork. They came from an old source, namely Randolph Hearst's collection. Hearst died in 1951, leaving the National Magazine Company with the problem of disposing not only of St Donat's Castle but also of quantities of objects of all shapes and sizes which had remained dismembered and packed ever since they had been purchased. Many of the architectural pieces had been sent across the Atlantic for possible use at San Simeon and then returned to St Donat's – one of Hearst's biographers quotes a comment that a large part of the world's tonnage was used in shipping Hearst oddments back and forth across the seas.

The agent for the National Magazine Company was Murray Adams-Acton, to whom over the years so many letters came from Burrell that his wife used to call him his boyfriend – Burrell would not have been amused by this. Adams-Acton himself wrote a number of amusing letters in connection with the disposal of the Hearst items (he reckoned that with his commission he could just about afford some new

Seven of the roundels from Vale Royal (opposite page):

(a) Arms of King Henry VIII.
(b) Arms of King Henry VIII and his wife Jane Seymour.
(c) Arms of Henry Fitzalan, Earl of Arundel.
(d) Arms of Edward Stanley, 3rd Earl of Derby.
(e) Arms of William Paulet, Earl of Wiltshire.
(f) Arms of Booth
(g) Arms of Sir William Venables.

See plate 29

boots!) but it was by no means an easy task, even at the knock-down prices that were being asked for panelling, fireplaces, medieval stone portals and windows. Undoubtedly their cheapness was an important consideration so far as Burrell was concerned, but what must have appealed most of all was the impact such large items would have on the appearance of the as yet undesigned galley to house the Collection. It is likely that Adams-Acton was instrumental in implanting the idea in Burrell's mind, especially as almost immediately afterwards he produced his designs for the building. Nonetheless Burrell's decision to acquire the large architectural stonework by any standards showed great foresight; it was especially remarkable in an old man into his nineties.

The Hearst material was bought in four separate lots, excluding some good armour which was purchased from the same source. The first came in August 1952 and included a polychromed linenfold screen from the great hall at Beaudesert in Staffordshire, a ceiling of *c*.1500 with elaborately carved bosses from Bridgewater in Somerset, some linenfold panelling with Renaissance details from the former Neptune Inn at Ipswich and an East Anglian church screen. The price amounted to £3,000. The second lot was acquired fifteen months later and included four medieval stone doorways and a magnificent Elizabethan carved wooden mantelpiece reputedly from the royal palace at Oatlands near Weybridge, destroyed in the seventeenth century. Adams-Acton told Hannah that Burrell had bought this by telephone unseen. The most expensive item was the late twelfth-century portal from the church at Montron, near Château-Thierry, which cost a mere £550, much to Burrell's delight:

> It cost Hearst £4500 & was then sent to America. Later it was brought to St Donat's so that it has crossed the Atlantic twice and what between packing, freight, insurance, etc etc it must have cost Hearst about £5000. I bought it for £550.

The last two lots followed each other in quick succession in the summer of 1954. The first comprised a set of seven limestone doorways and windows in the best French Flamboyant style which had lain dismantled in their packing cases since Hearst had bought them in Paris before the Second World War; their price was £1,400. Among the last group were three windows and a doorway from Provence of *c*.1200, two fourteenth-century Flemish or German windows with elaborate tracery, and the enormous early sixteenth-century portal formerly giving access to the great hall of Hornby Castle in Yorkshire; elaborately carved with the arms of the Conyers family it was an absolute bargain at £150. The entire lot amounted to a mere £600, including the oak double doors for the main archway at Hornby. The carved stones for the archway itself were included *gratis* by Adams-Acton: this arch

See plate 31

The late 12th-century portal from Montron purchased from the Hearst Collection for a fraction of the price paid by the American newspaper magnate. In the acquisition of monumental architectural items like this Burrell showed remarkable foresight.

together with its doors now form the public entrance to the Burrell Collection.

Burrell remained blissfully unaware of the enormous work undertaken variously by Adams-Acton, Hannah and the Glasgow Museums' staff in unpacking, measuring, transporting and storing such huge objects. Nor could he have anticipated the difficulties that would be encountered nearly thirty years later in incorporating them into the structure of the new building. The end result, however, justifies all the toil and trouble and there can be no two opinions regarding the effectiveness of the stone arches and portals, the Beaudesert screen and the Bridgewater ceiling, and the other items of architectural woodwork. They give an age and sense of permanence to the modern fabric of the building and act as a framework for the smaller exhibits.

By the time the purchases from the Hearst Collection had been completed Burrell was already bringing his collecting activities to a close. In 1954 only 72 items were added to the Collection, and the totals were even less in the following three years (50, 34, and 26 respectively). As 1954 progressed the first signs of physical deterioration became apparent. Burrell's handwriting started to get shaky and at the end of the year his eyesight was becoming so poor that he had to ask Andrew Hannah to use black ink in order to decipher his correspondence more easily. In spite of this handicap he continued to write almost all his letters (a few are in Lady Burrell and their daughter Marion's hands) and fill in the Purchase Book entries. Towards the end of 1956, by which time he was largely confined to bed, his handwriting became

almost illegible and he was forced to delegate the task to Marion and his housekeeper. All the entries in the last Purchase Book were made by these two.

At the same time Hutton Castle was gradually stripped of its valuable fittings and furnishings. The more portable items of the Collection were transferred to Glasgow first, in several large consignments. The process was completed by 1954. First of all came the rugs and tapestries and modern fabrics such as the lamp-shades and curtains. Then followed the larger items. In 1956 the medieval stained glass was removed from the dining room, drawing-room, hall and other principal rooms and was taken to Glasgow along with several large pieces of furniture. Soon after most of the remaining antique furniture, including needlework settees and chairs, were taken out, and early in 1958 the sixteenth-century panelling from Harrington Hall, which Burrell had had installed in the dining room at considerable expense, was transported to Glasgow. That left precious little for him and his wife and daughter to enjoy.

The atmosphere of neglect and austerity was compounded by the lack of domestic staff. Burrell's wants and needs became progressively fewer and Hutton was in the last years run on a shoe-string. Gone were the shooting parties and entertaining of the pre-war years, and for most of the time there was only a resident cook/housekeeper, with various

The Hutton Castle dining room in 1982: a photograph taken from the opposite end of the room to that on page 110.

estate cottages occupied by a chauffeur and gardener. So run down was the Castle that the staff of Glasgow Museums on their journeys to Hutton to collect objects were usually left to find accommodation and food in local hotels and inns.

Burrell was not one to follow Altman, Arabella Huntington, Kress and other clients of Joseph Duveen who continued to spend large sums when totally blind or nearly so. Early in 1956 he told Adams-Acton that he was ceasing to buy any more. Thereafter only a few Ancient Civilisations and Persian artefacts were acquired. The final entry is dated 22 June 1957, comprising five items of Persian pottery. The last of these is a ninth/tenth-century dish costing £15. Adams-Acton summed up Burrell's long career with perfect understatement when he told Hannah that his collecting was coming to an end:

If this be true . . . well . . . he has not done too badly!

Soon after even Sir William Burrell with all his tenacity and strong will had to bow to the inevitable. He died at Hutton Castle late on Saturday 29 March 1958, in his ninety-seventh year. A few days later he was buried, as were so many other members of the Burrell family, in the cemetery on the hill overlooking Largs and the Forth of Clyde, up and down which so many of his ships had sailed. The pomp and circumstance surrounding the interment of public figures was not what he wanted. The funeral, at his request, was a quiet family affair, with Glasgow represented solely by the Lord Provost and Bill Wells. His last remains were laid to rest in the spirit of modesty and privacy in which he had lived throughout his life. His grave is marked by a simple headstone, contrasting sharply with the more grandiose monuments of his father and of his brother George's family which stand nearby.

Burrell's last purchase: the Persian plate he bought for £15.

Epilogue:
The Search
For A Home
For The Collection

I cannot believe that there is another site more appropriate for the housing of this collection anywhere else in the world.

Richard Buchanan MP

LATE in 1954 Murray Adams-Acton penned a characteristically lively letter to Andrew Hannah. A passage on the subject of the eventual home for the Collection was not only amusing, it was also prophetic:

> I visualise a grand opening ceremony around the '75s with the Queen & you in yr frock coat, flowers & lillies, flashlights haggis & trumpets, when H.M. calls for a sword & (after a time) a double-handed weapon, having been produced from a case; the glass smashed, the key having been lost, H.M. says 'Arise Sir Andrew.' Should I be in the land of the living you can count upon a throaty cheer from a dusty corner before I am thrown out – then we'll have a drink together.

Although he rightly predicted the presence of royalty, even Adams-Acton did not anticipate that it would be nearly another decade after the mid-1970's before the Burrell Collection was finally opened to the public in a permanent home. When it took place neither Hannah nor Adams-Acton, nor any of the protagonists of the years following the Deed of Gift, was alive to see it.

At the time of Burrell's death the question of a suitable site was still unresolved. On two occasions, in September 1959 and a year later, Glasgow Corporation tried to persuade the Trustees of the Collection to agree to locate it within the city boundaries. Notwithstanding arguments that the operation of the Clean Air Act and the creation of smokeless zones rendered Sir William's stipulations of a rural site unnecessary from the conservation angle, the Trustees remained adamant that the original terms of the Deed of Gift had to be strictly adhered to. Thereafter the matter remained in abeyance for some years, in spite of periodic agitation in the correspondence and editorial columns of the press, usually accusing the Corporation of dilatoriness, and even of the formation of an action group called the Friends of the Burrell Collection, which disappeared as quickly as it had formed.

Meanwhile the gutting of Hutton Castle was completed after the death of Lady Burrell on 15 August 1961. The removal of the stone fireplaces and wooden pelmets together with the doors and lintels which had been installed at such expense little more than thirty years before left Hutton a shell which soon after began to deteriorate into the melancholy ruin it is today.

Once it was stored in Glasgow, Bill Wells was kept busy recording the Collection, a task which was greatly facilitated by the discovery of the Purchase Books, the very existence of which was unknown to anyone outside Hutton Castle. Their emergence owed everything to Wells' persistence. Fairly certain that as methodical a man as Burrell would have left a more accurate record of his acquisitions than the rather unhelpful inventory lists which he had furnished to Glasgow Museums and Art Galleries, Bill Wells paid a visit to the family lawyer soon after Lady Burrell's death. The office contained piles of documents and files removed from Hutton, but his enquiry as to whether there was anything relating to the Collection was answered in the negative. Just as Wells turned towards the door to leave he noticed a pile of exercise books. Having sighted his quarry and terrified that it might be mislaid he refused to leave empty-handed.

The Collection did not remain entirely hidden from public gaze. Until shortly before the gallery opened to the public the pick of the Old Masters and French nineteenth-century paintings hung at Kelvingrove, and almost every year until the late 1970's exhibitions of parts of it were held both there and in other Scottish galleries. Amongst the most notable were those devoted to the stained glass (in 1962 and 1965), for which Bill Wells wrote excellent catalogues. Several showings even took place in Edinburgh, which in the light of his steadfast refusal in his later years to have anything loaned there may well have caused Burrell to turn in his grave.

Loans were also made to special exhibitions, of which the most important were the *British Embroidery* show at Birmingham Museum and Art Gallery in 1959 and the *Degas 1879* exhibition at the National Gallery of Scotland twenty years later. Although the policy of long-term loans of individual items from the Collection had been discontinued in Burrell's last years an exception was made in the late 1970's, when some of the best oak furniture and other fittings were lent to the Leeds Castle Foundation; it is ironic that in this glorious Kent castle (which formed the setting for that most delicious of films *Kind Hearts and Coronets*) these pieces were more at home than they could ever have been at Hutton.

The Deed of Gift had never envisaged that the Collection should be a finite one after Burrell's death, although it did exclude outside bequests. Additions could be made, but only through his daughter or the Trustees; the only limitation Burrell imposed was that a decided preference should be given to works of art of the highest quality of his much-loved Gothic period. The Trustees of the Collection have used the money made available by him for this purpose only rarely, but when they have, some major acquisitions have been made, including two important tapestries woven around 1530 in Brussels, which were bought at Sotheby's shortly after Burrell's death. Together they cost the considerable sum of £9,100, but this was eclipsed twenty years later when within the space of a few weeks the Trustees made two major forays into the art market, which took one of the world's great museums by surprise and focussed international attention on the Collection. Among the numerous treasures of Warwick Castle which were put up for sale in 1978 by Lord Brooke the most spectacular was the huge Roman marble vase which had stood for two hundred years in the orangery at the Castle. It had been discovered in fragments during 1770–71 in the grounds of Hadrian's Villa near Tivoli by the Scottish painter Gavin Hamilton. He sold the pieces to Sir William Hamilton, whose renown as a collector of antiquities has been obscured by the affair of his wife Emma with Lord Nelson. Sir William had the Vase reconstructed and tried unsuccessfully to sell it to the British Museum. By 1778 it had passed to his nephew George Greville, Earl of Warwick; subsequently it formed the model for numerous sporting trophies, including the Colgate PGA rose bowl and the Grand Challenge Cup of Henley Royal Regatta, as well as providing the subject matter for numerous pottery designs. The Vase was acquired by a consortium of art dealers who sold it to New York's Metropolitan Museum of Art for £253,808. The Reviewing Committee for the Export of Works of Art put a temporary embargo on the transaction and literally at the eleventh hour negotiations were concluded which enabled the Vase to be purchased by the Trustees of the Burrell Collection with the aid of generous support from the Scottish Heritage Fund, the National Art-Collections Fund and the Carnwath Trust. Once acquired for the Collection the Vase was put on show to the public in the Museum of Transport at Glasgow, the only one of the city's museums capable of withstanding its nine tons weight, before its present installation in the courtyard of the Burrell Collection gallery.

Just how close a shave it had been became apparent to me when shortly afterwards I visited the Metropolitan. Colleagues there related how a place for the Vase had already been designated and the report

recording its purchase had been typed and was about to be included in the papers for a meeting of the Museum's Trustees that afternoon, when a telegram was received with the news that the Burrell Collection, not the Metropolitan, was to be its final home. The price would have horrified Sir William Burrell.

He might also have cavilled at the £34,000 (excluding buyer's premium and commission) which the Trustees paid at the same time for two panels of early fifteenth-century English stained glass depicting the Annunciation and Assumption of the Virgin, although he may have been reconciled to it by their superb quality. The panels originally came from Hampton Court in Herefordshire and were the finest English glass to be seen on the market for many years. Once again the Metropolitan Museum was unlucky: it wanted them for display in the Cloisters in Fort Tryon Park, and so certain had the staff been of outbidding competitors that packing cases had even been sent over to London. In a world of intense rivalry between public museums it was a rare victory for the Old World over the New, but only slight revenge for the loss to the Cloisters of the superb twelfth-century ivory known as the *Bury Cross*, the competition for which between various American institutions and the British Museum is colourfully related by the Metropolitan's former Director Tom Hoving in *King of the Confessors* (London, 1981).

By the time both the *Warwick Vase* and the Hampton Court panels were acquired, construction work on their eventual home had at long last got underway. To have attained this goal entailed following a path strewn with pitfalls and in negotiating it the Corporation endured many accusations of feet-dragging – headlines like 'The Great Art Scandal' and 'Will the "Burrell" ever find a home?' were all too common. To some extent the criticism was justified; for a city like Glasgow its social and housing problems must be more pressing than those of a new art gallery, and in these circumstances for the elected representatives and officials the Burrell issue was a millstone around their necks. The problem, as ever, lay in Burrell's insistence that the Collection had to be housed sixteen miles from the city centre, a condition that the Corporation officials had foreseen from the outset would be a major handicap. His Trustees for their part felt themselves bound to see that the Deed of Gift was respected. With the benefit of hindsight it can be said that in the years following Burrell's death the Corporation might have pressed the Trustees to ameliorate the terms because of cleaner atmospheres and developments in air-conditioning. Their attention might also have been drawn to the fact that even during Burrell's lifetime the conditions of the Deed of Gift were with his own consent broken, firstly in his agreeing to the display of the sensitive tapestries in the McLellan Galleries on two occasions, in 1949 and 1951 (the Trustees themselves consented to showing the tapestries in urban environments on several occasions), and more importantly in his enthusiasm for the Dougalston and Mugdock sites. It is particularly regrettable that a letter from Burrell to Hannah written in March 1948 in which he expressed his willingness to alter the distance conditions went unnoticed.

In the event the issue remained deadlocked until 1963. In March of that year the Standing Commission on Museums and Art Galleries took the Corporation and the Trustees firmly to task in its annual report. The Commission described the Burrell Collection as the most serious problem of all the United Kingdom museums which required a new building. It regretted that the difficulty of finding a site for 'this immense and priceless collection of national importance' was not over-come in Burrell's lifetime. The Commission was convinced that 'only a sufficient degree of enthusiasm and determination' was needed to break the deadlock. 'Nothing could be more obviously contrary to Sir William's intentions than the present deplorable situation.' The Corporation should regard the resolution of the problem as 'a compelling debt of honour'. The Chairman of the Commission, the Earl of Rosse, did not mince his words when he backed up the Report with this statement:

> This is a national scandal. It is the most severe lapse that we have discovered in the course of our investigations. Here we have this magnificent collection which has been languishing in packing cases for the past 20 years without anyone having the backbone to do something about it . . . we feel that all concerned – by that we mean Glasgow Corporation and the Burrell Trustees – must put their heads together and get down to sorting out a solution right away.
>
> (Daily Express, 20 March 1963)

Stung by this rebuke, the Corporation in the person of the Lord Provost, Peter Meldrum, shortly after took the first steps towards resolving the *impasse*. He suggested that the building to house the Collection should be sited in the 360-acre Pollok Estate, on the south side of Glasgow. Although only three miles from the city centre, this proposal was in accordance with Burrell's strongly expressed desire for a rural setting and from the Corporation's point of view it overcame the disadvantages of administering a building far beyond the city boundaries.

Pollok Estate has been connected with the Stirling Maxwell family for more than seven hundred years. At its centre lies Pollok House, an elegant small-scale country seat built between *c*.1750 and 1752, with wings and entrance hall added in a harmonious style at the turn of the last century. Sir John Stirling Maxwell, 10th Baronet (1866–1956), was responsible for creating the superb gardens, and particularly the rhododendrons, which make the Estate such a popular attraction and enable visitors to forget instantly that they have just left busy city roads and dense housing. His father, Sir William Stirling Maxwell (1818–78), built up a fine collection of Spanish paintings, including works by El Greco, Goya and Murillo, as well as pictures by Signorelli, Sebastiano del Piombo and others and much furniture and silver. In his liking for Southern artists his tastes were very different from Burrell's and as he owned an eighteenth-century house (a period in which Burrell was not very interested, apart from British portraiture), here was an opportunity to see the gatherings of two major collectors which complemented rather than clashed with each other.

There was, therefore, everything to recommend this suggestion. Moreover the timing was propitious, for Sir John's daughter, Mrs Anne Maxwell Macdonald, with great generosity was in the process of ensuring the preservation of the Estate by offering it and Pollok House to the National Trust for Scotland. The Maxwell Macdonald family was fully in sympathy with locating the Burrell Collection within the Estate and so was the National Trust. This still left a major hurdle, the Trustees of the Collection. In view of the past abortive negotiations the Corporation officials approached them with no great hopes of success, but in the event their fears were unjustified. The meeting was recalled by Richard Buchanan, Labour MP for Springburn, during a debate on the Burrell Collection in the House of Commons in May 1966:

> On 16 December 1963, the trustees, those concerned in the National Trust, and ourselves visited the Pollok estate. On that grey December day Pollok estate still looked gorgeous. The trustees were impressed. They considered, they held meetings, and they agreed, subject to certain safeguards and conditions, that the Burrell Collection should be housed in Pollok. . . . I cannot believe that there is another site more appropriate for the housing of this collection anywhere else in the world.

These 'certain safeguards and conditions' were concerned with the installation of modern air-conditioning and having satisfied themselves on this subject the Trustees left the way clear. At this juncture certain obstacles not directly concerned with the Burrell Collection presented themselves, which prompted the Parliamentary debate. By an agreement made with Sir John Stirling Maxwell, Glasgow Corporation had a right of pre-emption on Pollok Estate in the event of its disposal by the family, and some members of the majority Labour group amongst the city councillors were strongly opposed to its transfer to the National Trust, preferring to see it in municipal ownership. Secondly the National Trust itself required a large endowment for the maintenance of Pollok House and its contents together with the Estate and applied to the Treasury for a sum of £350,000. This was not forthcoming and eventually at the end of 1967 Mrs Maxwell Macdonald presented Pollok House and Estate to the City of Glasgow. A site for the new Burrell Collection building was selected in the Picnic Field, a pasture area sloping towards the south and screened by woodland from Pollok House. A statement was made in Parliament that the Government would make a contribution of £250,000 towards the cost. It was thought at the time that the new building could not be erected for much less than £4 million. After taking into account this grant and Burrell's original sum of £450,000 which with accrued interest had risen to £750,000, this left the Corporation with the task of finding some £3 million. Nonetheless the Corporation decided to press ahead and in 1968 announced that it would hold a competition, to be sponsored by the Royal Institute of British Architects, to find a suitable design. This decision met with general approval, although Tom Honeyman was a notable voice of dissent, holding that a Glasgow architect should be appointed who would design a much cheaper building more in accordance with Burrell's own wishes. Honeyman may well have recalled a letter he received from Sir William in 1949: 'To put up an extravagant building is quite opposed to what we have stipulated.'

The Trustees, the National Trust and the Corporation officials were all aware of what was at stake. No museum on such a scale had been built in the British Isles in the twentieth century and the particular issues of siting and layout demanded a design which would show the contents to best advantage, harmonise with the landscape and reconcile the requirements of conservation and security.

A team of assessors was appointed to prepare a brief and adjudicate on the designs. The team consisted of four architects, all members of well-known practices in London and Glasgow, and Lord Muirshiel, a former Secretary of State for Scotland, who represented the Burrell Trustees, the Maxwell Macdonald family, Nether Pollok Ltd and the National Trust for Scotland; the Principal of Glasgow University, Sir Charles Wilson, was the nominee of Glasgow Corporation. Over the next two years the brief was prepared. The assessors visited newly-built museums and art galleries, including the Gulbenkian in Lisbon. Bill Wells and the small Burrell staff worked out the display and storage requirements of the Collection and also arranged exhibitions at Kelvingrove of major parts, including carpets and tapestries, for the benefit of both the assessors and competitors.

The brief was published in September 1970. It contained a series of conditions and bound the Corporation to appoint the winner as the architect for the work. The sum to be expended was put at £2,500,000, based on current costs of labour and materials. The brief went into considerable details regarding the categories of the Collection and number of pieces to be displayed. Attention was drawn in particular to the Hutton drawing-room, dining room and hall, and to the large medieval stone arches and doorways which Burrell had acquired from Randolph Hearst's collection. This stonework was illustrated, together with a representative range of items in the Collection, including pictures, sculptures, tapestries, carpets and stained glass.

Altogether 242 entries were received, including one which was so much in sympathy with the pastoral nature of the setting that it took the form of a cow. Not surprisingly this was not one of the six short-listed designs for the second stage of the competition. These included submissions from leading architects of international repute like Denys Lasdun & Partners, who subsequently built the National Theatre complex on the South Bank. The eventual winners, announced in March 1972, were a team of unknown young architects, Barry Gasson, John Meunier and Brit Andresen, all tutors in the Cambridge University School of Architecture. Their design won universal acceptance. In the assessors' words it was 'an unqualified winner . . . a richly worked out

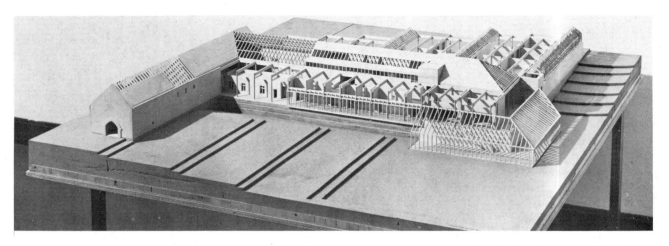

Model of the winning design for the Burrell Collection building, made around 1975.

and elegant solution . . . quite outstanding in both its practicability and its originality.' Unlike the other finalists they fully exploited the natural possibilities presented by the site and instead of imposing an alien element conspicuously in the middle of the field minimised its impact by placing the building in the west corner, against the woodlands. This had the merit of reducing and harmonising its scale. Again in the words of the assessors, the juxtaposing of the glass north wall against the tree-line '. . . brings about a direct relationship between the collection and the natural setting, and provides a constant identifying element and a marvellously varying seasonal component to the interior.' The design was unmistakeably modern and the antithesis of the neo-classical miniature British Museum envisaged twenty years earlier by both Murray Adams-Acton and Frank Surgey. But as the Glasgow Herald remarked in an editorial, it 'bears the mark of one designed for the benefit of the contents rather than outward appearance. . . . Too many museums, behind an elegant façade, have little of help to the curators who wish to display exhibits to advantage.'

Whatever the intrinsic merits of the scheme there still remained a strong possibility that it would go the way of many other competition winners and remain no more than a series of plans and elevations. The reason, as ever, was the soaring cost of the project. A year after the results of the competition were announced inflation had raised the final estimated cost from £5.8 million to £8.2 million. The Corporation had no option but to approach the Government to increase substantially its agreed contribution of £250,000. It was not a good moment, for the Secretary of State for Scotland was now also under pressure to approve a new £4 million building for the National Museum of Antiquities in Edinburgh. In the harsh economic climate then prevailing it was obvious that the Minister was not going to give the go-ahead to both schemes and would have to choose between them.

The issue hung delicately in the balance for three years while the interested parties lobbied strongly and the Government vacillated. At

the beginning of August 1976 the Secretary of State, Bruce Millan, pronounced in favour of the Burrell Collection and promised a 50% grant of the net cost. There can be little doubt that a splendid piece of opportunism by Trevor Walden, appointed Director of Glasgow Museums and Art Galleries in December 1971, played an important part in influencing this decision. He learned that a gap had unexpectedly occurred in the programme of exhibitions planned for the Hayward Gallery on the South Bank in London and immediately stepped in with an offer to show a selection from the Burrell Collection. Barry Gasson and John Meunier together with the Arts Council designed the exhibition, appropriately entitled *Treasures from the Burrell Collection*, which ran for six weeks early in 1975. It was widely acclaimed and the enthusiastic reviews in leading art journals and newspapers drew

Artist's impression of the interior of the gallery from the east end of the north gallery, made around 1975.

The exhibition TREASURES FROM THE BURRELL COLLECTION at the Hayward Gallery in 1975: it did much to draw national attention to the lack of a permanent home for the Collection.

attention nation-wide to the as yet unsettled long-term fate of the Collection. It is ironic to think that an exhibition which played such an important rôle in securing the Collection's permanent home in Pollok Park took place on one of the very sites Burrell had considered when he was pondering to whom he should entrust his treasures. Further publicity was obtained shortly before the Secretary of State's announcement, when a documentary on Burrell narrated by Magnus Magnusson was shown on BBC television. It was here that the phrase 'the Millionaire Magpie' was coined.

With the Secretary of State's grant secured, building could at long last proceed. Competitive tenders were obtained and the contract was won by Taylor Woodrow (Scotland) Ltd. Even at the very last minute there was another of those hitches which had bedevilled the project for so long. A ceremony was arranged for 4 May 1978, at which Princess Margaret was to press the starter button of a bulldozer to inaugurate work on the site, but at the eleventh hour the Princess had to cancel her visit because of illness. It would have been hard to find a more appropriate replacement than Sir William's own daughter and she performed the ceremony perfectly.

One crucial question which frequently comes to mind is whether Sir William Burrell would have approved of the final home for his collection (a less charitable thought is that in the light of the problems with Hutton Castle the tasks of both architect and Keeper would have been made significantly more difficult had he lived through its planning and construction). The question must perforce remain unanswered, but a comment made by Andrew Hannah to Frank Surgey nearly twenty-five years ago gives grounds for thinking that Burrell would have given it his blessing:

> I anticipate criticism from him [Burrell] regarding any building which is not 20th Century both in its interior and exterior aspects. He seems to be strongly against any kind of reconstructed or pseudo-period building. . . .

The home at last achieved: the Burrell Collection gallery in Pollok Park, photographed in May 1983, when preparations for the opening were still going on.
(DSB Photographic Services)

SOURCES

INTRODUCTION

The most useful material is to be found amongst the correspondence in the Burrell Collection archives. Tom Honeyman's *Art and Audacity* (p. 141) is the source of the last quotation; the same author recounted the A.J. McNeill Reid anecdote about Burrell's abilities as a raconteur in an article in the *Scottish Field* (June 1958), p. 39. The evidence of Burrell's former office boys is taken from the Glasgow Herald of 5 July 1977. Lord Clark's description of Burrell as an aesthete and his rôle in the purchase of the Bellini appear in his 'Sir William Burrell – A Personal Reminiscence' (see Bibliography). Mrs Hearst's comments on her husband are taken from Swanberg's biography of Hearst (see Bibliography), p. 468.

1: BURRELL AND SON

The family's Northumbrian origins have been traced from *A History of Northumberland*, vol. ii, by E. Bateson (London and Newcastle upon Tyne, 1895); vol. vii, ed. J.C. Hodgson (London and Newcastle upon Tyne, 1904); vol. xiv, ed. M.H. Dods (Newcastle upon Tyne, 1935). Particularly informative as it includes a Burrell family tree is J.C. Hodgson, 'The Manor and Township of Shipley', *Archaeologia Aeliana*, 3rd series vol. xx (1923), pp. 1–27.

The major source for the early history of Burrell and Son is the four articles in *Sea Breezes* (see Bibliography) by David Burrell, who has also provided further information in correspondence. Dr John Cage also generously made available the results of his preliminary researches on the history of the firm. The observations by the Rioch brothers were taken from the BBC television documentary 'The Millionaire Magpie'. Lorimer's letters to R.S. Dods are published in Dr Peter Savage's articles on Burrell in *Country Life* (see Bibliography). Information on the Forth & Clyde Canal came from C.A. Pratt, *Scottish Canals and Waterways* (London, 1922); details on the Hamiltonhill shipyard were taken from a file in the Glasgow Museum of Transport, G.W. Burrows, *Puffer*

Ahoy! (Glasgow, 1981) and D. McDonald, *The Clyde Puffer* (London, 1977). Works consulted on Scottish shipping include J. Hume and M.S. Moss, *Clyde Shipbuilding from Old Photographs* (London, 1975), R.S. McLellan, *The Anchor Line 1856–1956* (Glasgow, 1956), A.A. McAlister, *H. Hogarth & Son Ltd – A Short History* (Kendal, 1976), G. Blake, *The Ben Line* (London, 1956); the study by A. Muir and M. Davies of Charles William Cayzer, *A Victorian Shipowner* (privately published, 1978) was particularly useful. For the general economic and social background to Victorian Glasgow, C.E. Oakley, *'The Second City'* (Glasgow and London, 3rd ed. 1975) and D. Daiches, *Glasgow* (London, 1977) have been consulted.

Amongst the original sources used are a Burrell family pedigree in the archives of the Burrell Collection, the Census Returns for 1861 and 1871 and Glasgow Post Office Directories. Other letters and information were supplied by members of the Burrell family, Dr Ronald Cant and Mrs Frank Surgey.

2: THE GLASGOW SCENE

For Glasgow collectors, A. Kay, *Treasure Trove in Art* (Edinburgh and London, 1939) and the sale catalogues of the Sir Thomas Gibson Carmichael (1902) and W.A. Coats (1927) Collections have been consulted; further information on Kay is to be found in the Bailie (20 March 1901) and *Who's Who in Glasgow in 1909*, and on W.A. Coats in C. Thompson, *Pictures for Scotland: The National Gallery of Scotland and its Collection* (Edinburgh, 1972). Obituaries of T.G. Arthur (1907), Coats (1926) and Kay (1939) are in the Glasgow Herald. Alexander Reid has been the subject of a Scottish Arts Council exhibition *A Man of Influence Alex Reid 1854–1928* (see Bibliography), which also has information on Craibe Angus. There is a valuable introduction to the sale catalogue of Cottier's collection (Edinburgh, 1892), and his early career is summarised in M. Donnelly, *Glasgow Stained Glass – a Preliminary Study* (Glasgow, 1981). B. Gould, *Two Van Gogh Contacts: E.L. Van Wisselingh, art dealer; Daniel Cottier, glass-painter and decorator* (Naples Press, London, 1969) is also useful.

3: EARLY COLLECTING

The chief evidence for Burrell's collecting before 1916 is the *Official Catalogue of the Glasgow International Exhibition of 1901* (Glasgow, 1901) and the early Purchase Books. The primary reference work on the Glasgow Boys is the two-volume Catalogue of the Scottish Arts Council exhibition which was held in 1971; Burrell's Whistler purchases are mentioned in N. Munro, *The Brave Days* (Edinburgh, 1931) and A. McLaren Young, M. McDonald, R. Spencer, H. Miles, *The Paintings of James McNeill Whistler* (Yale, 1980). For the Daumiers see R. Pickvance, 'Daumier in Scotland – 1', *Scottish Art Review* 12, No 1 (1969), pp. 13–16, 29. The source for the acquisition of the Isabella d'Andreini porcelain figurine is W. Muirhead Moffat, 'Portrait of my Father – Part II', *Scottish Art Review*, 14, No 4 (1975), p.24.

Other works consulted include J. Lavery, *The Life of a Painter* (London, 1940) and Peter Savage's publications on Lorimer to which reference was made in the first chapter. The pictures auctioned by Burrell in 1902 are listed in Christie's Sale Catalogues of 16 May, lots 137–158, and 14 June, lots 1–17. Further information has been obtained from the Burrell Collection archives, members of the Burrell family, Mrs Gertrude Hunt and Christopher Lorimer.

4: HUTTON CASTLE

Burrell's purchase of and alterations to Hutton are comparatively well-documented. The early history and architecture of the Castle are recorded in D.S. Leslie, *Notes on Hutton Castle* (Berwick-on-Tweed, 1934), D. MacGibbon and T. Ross, *The Castellated and Domestic Architecture of Scotland*, Vol. IV (Edinburgh, 1892), and the Royal Commission on Ancient and Historical Monuments of Scotland, *6th Report and Inventory of Monuments and Constructions in the County of Berwick* (Edinburgh, 1915). Further details, especially of Lord Tweedmouth's alterations, are taken from the 1915 sale prospectus for the Estate which includes valuable photographs of the Castle. The original correspondence between Lorimer and Burrell is in the Lorimer papers deposited in Edinburgh University Library (file Gen. 1963/6/270–299), and Lorimer's drawings for Hutton are in the National Monuments Record of Scotland. Other information on Lorimer is taken from P. Savage, *Lorimer and the Edinburgh Craft Designers* (Edinburgh, 1980). Other published sources include Lord Clark, 'Sir William Burrell – A Personal Reminiscence' (see Bibliography) and C. McWilliam, *The Buildings of Scotland: Lothian* (Harmondsworth, 1978). Details of Queen Mary's visit to Hutton are recorded in the Berwick Journal & North Northumberland News (11 September 1930, p. 10). The Purchase Books and correspondence (especially that between Burrell and Wilfred Drake) in the Burrell Collection archives have also yielded valuable information. Mr J.A. Houston, Mrs Julia Turbitt, Frank Whyte and relatives of Sir William provided details of life at Hutton.

5: BETWEEN THE WARS

This chapter is based mainly on the Purchase Books and Burrell's correspondence in the archives of the Collection. The Wilfred Drake letters in the archives have also proved informative. G. Reitlinger, *The Economics of Taste*, 2 vols. (London, 1963) provided the background to the art market in this period and for Duveen and Hearst the biographies of S.N. Behrman and W.A. Swanberg were valuable as well as entertaining (see Bibliography). *The Antiquaries Journal*, XXXIII (1953), p. 274 provided a brief biography of Philip Nelson and the author is grateful to Dick Randall for his observations on Henry Walters. The account of J. Paul Getty's purchasing policy is taken from an article by Russell Miller in The Sunday Times Magazine for 24 April 1983, p. 22. For Pitcairn the Metropolitan Museum of Art exhibition catalogue, *Radiance and Reflection – Medieval Art from the Raymond Pitcairn Collection* (1982) was consulted. The extract regarding Burrell's first visit to Seligmann's premises is taken from G. Seligman, *Merchants of Art*, pp. 200–1. The account of John Hunt is based on the obituary in the *North Munster Antiquarian Journal*, XVIII (1976), J.P.F. Doran, *The Hunt Museum* (see Bibliography) and the reminiscences of Mrs Hunt. For Frank Partridge see the article in *The Connoisseur*, vol. 213 No. 851, listed in the Bibliography. John Partridge kindly provided the account of Burrell's first visit and Leslie Dawson recounted his views on oak furniture. Other anecdotes and information were provided by Colin Thompson (National Galleries of Scotland), Mandy Green (Tate Gallery Archive), Lord Eccles, Patrick Taylor, Peter Vaughan and Arnold Zwemmer.

The main primary document for the donation of the Collection to Glasgow is a copy of the Memorandum of Agreement in the archives of the Burrell Collection. The report of the British Antiques Dealers Association dinner is taken from a press cutting in The Times in the possession of Mrs Frank Surgey, who also provided information on the suggestion *vis à vis* St John's Lodge in Regent's Park. The details of other possible sites in and around London are taken from Lord Clark's 'Sir William Burrell – A Personal Reminiscence' (see Bibliography). The reference to East Barsham occurs in the correspondence with Wilfred Drake in the Burrell Collection archives. The account of the negotiations with Glasgow is based on Tom Honeyman's *Art and Audacity* (see Bibliography).

6: THE LAST YEARS

The material used for this chapter is taken almost entirely from the Purchase Books and correspondence files. Other information has been provided by Mrs Hunt, Janet Notman, Mrs Surgey, Frank Whyte and Bill Wells, and from obituaries of Burrell in the Berwick Advertiser (3 April 1958) and the Scotsman (31 March 1958). The account of Burrell's reaction to the Dougalston proposal is taken from an article by Tom Honeyman in the Glasgow Herald (25 August 1968). For the post-war art market G. Reitlinger, *The Economics of Taste* (see Bibliography) was useful. Full descriptions of the Fawsley, Vale Royal and Blithfield glass can be found in Bill Wells' two catalogues of the stained glass in the Burrell Collection.

EPILOGUE: THE SEARCH FOR A HOME FOR THE COLLECTION

Almost all the information in this chapter is derived from the correspondence files in the Burrell Collection archives and contemporary reports and articles in the local and national Press. Richard Buchanan's account of the meeting in Pollok Park with the Burrell Trustees is taken from *Hansard*, 11 May 1966, pp. 550–551 and Tom Honeyman's views on the appointment of the architect occur on p. 155 of his *Art and Audacity*. There is a detailed survey by the assessors of the designs of the finalists, together with the latter's own comments in the *Architects Journal* (22 March 1972), pp. 590–602. For the *Warwick Vase* see the Glasgow Museums and Art Galleries publication by R. Marks and B. Blench (see Bibliography).

SELECTED BIBLIOGRAPHY

SIR WILLIAM BURRELL

The Bailie, No 1568 (5 Nov 1902).
D. Burrell, 'Burrell's Straths', *Sea Breezes*, 49 (1975), pp. 213–22, 271–80, 329–38, 388–96.
K. Clark 'Sir William Burrell – A Personal Reminiscence', *The Scottish Review*, 2, No 6 (Spring 1977), pp. 15–16.
T.J. Honeyman, *Art and Audacity*, Glasgow, 1971.
Lefevre Gallery exhib. cat., *Alex Reid and Lefevre 1926–1976*, London, 1976.
R. Marks, *Sir William Burrell 1861–1958*, Glasgow Museums and Art Galleries, 1982.
P. Savage, *Lorimer and the Edinburgh Craft Designers*, Edinburgh, 1980.
P. Savage, 'Through the Eyes of a Friend, William Burrell, Collector (1861–1958)', *Country Life* (January 27, 1977), pp. 194–6, (February 3, 1977), pp. 262–4.
G. Seligman, *Merchants of Art*, New York, 1961, pp. 201–3.
W. Wells, 'Sir William Burrell and his Collection', *Museums Journal*, 72 (1972), pp. 101–3.
W. Wells, 'Sir William Burrell', in *Treasures from the Burrell Collection*, exhibition catalogue, Arts Council 1975, pp. 6–11.
W. Wells, 'Sir William Burrell, the collectors' collector', *Hand-in-Hand* (the International Journal of Commercial Union Assurance), 2, No 6 (December 1977), pp. 9–15.
W. Wells, 'Sir William Burrell's Purchase Books', *Scottish Art Review*, 9 (1963), pp. 19–22 (reprinted in F. Herrmann, *The English as Collectors*, London, 1972, pp. 413–7).

HIS COLLECTION

A comprehensive bibliography on the Collection is to be found in the Arts Council exhibition catalogue, *Treasures from the Burrell Collection*, London, 1975, pp. 49–51.

The most significant publications since then are:

Arts Council exhibition catalogue, *The Burrell Collection Medieval Tapestries, Sculpture, etc.*, London, 1977.

The Burrell Collection 19th Century French Paintings, London, 1977.

National Galleries of Scotland exhibition catalogue, *Degas 1879*, Edinburgh, 1979.

R. Marks and B. Blench, *The Warwick Vase*, Glasgow Museums and Art Galleries, 1979.

OTHER COLLECTIONS AND COLLECTORS

General

S.N. Behrman, *Duveen*, London, 1972 (N.B. This is very informative on American collectors, including Morgan and Hearst).

F. Herrmann, *The English as Collectors*, London, 1972.

G. Seligman, *Merchants of Art*, New York, 1961 (also informative on American collectors).

Sir Alan Barlow

M. Sullivan, *Chinese Ceramics, Bronzes and Jades in the Collection of Sir Alan and Lady Barlow*, London, 1963.

Fritz Mayer Van Den Bergh

J. de Coo, *Fritz Mayer Van den Bergh*, Schoten, 1981.

Sir Thomas Gibson Carmichael

The Collection of Works of Art of Sir T. Gibson Carmichael Bart. (Christie's, Manson & Woods, sale catalogues of 12–13 May, 1902).

William Allen Coats

Catalogue of Pictures and Drawings being the entire Collection of the late W.A. Coats Esquire (Wm. B. Paterson, 5 Old Bond Street, London, W1), January, 1927.

C. Thompson, *Pictures for Scotland: The National Gallery of Scotland and its Collection*, Edinburgh, 1972, p. 85.

Sir Percival David

Illustrated Catalogue of the Percival David Foundation of Chinese Art, Section 1 – by S. Yorke Hardy, Section 2 – by Lady David, Sections 3–7 – by M. Medley, (1953–1980).

Leonard Gow

R.L. Hobson, *The Leonard Gow Collection of Chinese Porcelain*, London, 1931.

William Randolph Hearst

W.A. Swanberg, *Citizen Hearst*, London, 1961.

Robert Von Hirsch

Sotheby Parke Benet sale catalogue, *The Robert von Hirsch Collection*, 4 Vols, London, 1978.

Arthur Kay

The Bailie No 1483, (20 March 1901).

Treasure Trove in Art, Edinburgh and London, 1939.

Who's Who in Glasgow, 1909.

William Hesketh Lever

M. Medley, 'Chinese Art in the Lady Lever Art Gallery, Port Sunlight', *Transactions of the Oriental Ceramic Society*, 44 (1979–80), pp. 1–14.

J. Pierpont Morgan

A. Sinclair, *Corsair, The Life of J. Pierpont Morgan*, London, 1981.

F.H. Taylor, *Pierpont Morgan as Collector and Patron, 1873–1913*, New York, The Pierpont Morgan Library, 1970.

Raymond Pitcairn

Metropolitan Museum of Art exhibition catalogue, *Radiance and Reflection – Medieval Art from the Raymond Pitcairn Collection*, New York, 1982.

Alexander Schnütgen

Das Schnütgen – Museum Eine Auswahl, 4th ed, Cologne, 1968.

Henry Walters

G. Seligman, *Merchants of Art, op. cit.*

DEALERS

General

G. Reitlinger, *The Economics of Taste*, 2 vols, London, 1963.

J.R. Taylor and B. Brooke, *The Art Dealers*, London, 1969.

Daniel Cottier

Collection Cottier Catalogue (the sale was in Paris), Edinburgh, 1892.

B. Gould, *Two Van Gogh Contacts: E.J. Van Wisselingh, art dealer; Daniel Cottier, glass painter and decorator*, London, 1969.

Wilfred Drake

Obituary in *Journal of the British Society of Master Glass-Painters*, **X**, No 2 (1949), p. 105.

Joseph Duveen

S.N. Behrman, *Duveen*, London, 1972.

E. Fowles, *Memories of Duveen Brothers*, London, 1976.

John Hunt

J.P.F. Doran, *The Hunt Museum, The Craggaunowen Project*, Limerick/Shannon, 1981.

Obituary by the Very Revd Canon Culhane in *North Munster Antiquarian Journal*, **XVIII** (1976), pp. 93–4.

Frank Partridge

J. Durden-Smith, and D. de Simone, 'The Partridge Phenomenon', *Connoisseur*, 213, No 851 (January 1983), pp. 62–72.

Memoirs of the Late Frank Partridge, privately published, 1961.

Alexander Reid

T.J. Honeyman, *Art and Audacity*, Glasgow, 1971.

Lefevre Gallery exhibition catalogue, *Alex Reid and Lefevre 1926–1976*, London, 1976.

R. Pickvance, 'A Man of Influence: Alex Reid (1854–1928)', *Scottish Art Review*, 11 (1968), pp. 5–9.

Scottish Arts Council exhibition catalogue, *A Man of Influence: Alex Reid 1854–1928*, Edinburgh, 1967.

Grosvenor Thomas

Obituary in *Journal of the British Society of Master Glass-Painters*, 1, No 1 (1924), pp. 29–31.

Scottish Arts Council exhibition catalogue, *The Glasgow Boys 1880–1900*, 2 vols, Glasgow, 1971.

David Croal Thomson

A. Weil, 'David Croal Thomson: Spokesman for Art', *Scottish Art Review*, 14 (1975), pp. 3–5, 27.

E.J. Van Wisselingh

See under Daniel Cottier.

THE BURRELL COLLECTION BUILDING

'Burrell Collection Competition', *Architects Journal* (22 March 1972), pp. 590–602, (29 March 1972), pp. 104–106.

B. Gasson, 'Notes on the building for the Burrell Collection', *Museums Journal*, 72 (1972), pp. 104–106.

B. Gasson, 'Notes on the building for the Burrell Collection, Pollok Park, Glasgow', *Treasures from the Burrell Collection* exhib. cat. Arts Council, 1975, pp. 117–123.

'Burrell Museum takes shape' *Taywood News* (the house magazine of the Taylor Woodrow team of companies), 20, No 4 (April 1981), pp. 3–5.

P. Davey, 'Museum Piece', *Architects Journal* (9 February 1983), pp. 20–22.